Marxist Esthetics

MARXIST ESTHETICS

by HENRI ARVON

*Translated from the French
by Helen R. Lane*

✦

*With an Introduction
by Fredric Jameson*

CORNELL PAPERBACKS

Cornell University Press

ITHACA AND LONDON

L'esthetique marxiste, by Henri Arvon, first published
1970, copyright 1970, by Presses Universitaires de France

English language edition copyright © 1973 by Cornell University

All rights reserved. Except for brief quotations in a review, this book, or parts thereof, must not be reproduced in any form without permission in writing from the publisher. For information address Cornell University Press, 124 Roberts Place, Ithaca, New York 14850.

First published 1973 by Cornell University Press.
Published in the United Kingdom by Cornell University
Press Ltd., 2–4 Brook Street, London W1Y 1AA.

First printing, Cornell Paperbacks, 1973

International Standard Book Number 0-8014-9142-8
Library of Congress Catalog Card Number 72-12405

Printed in the United States of America by Vail-Ballou Press, Inc.

*Librarians: Library of Congress cataloging information
appears on the last page of the book.*

Contents

Introduction, by Fredric Jameson	vii
1. Marxism and Art	1
2. Dialectics	24
3. Form and Content	41
4. Revolutionary Art	56
5. The German Revolutionary Theater	71
6. Socialist Realism	83
7. Bertolt Brecht and George Lukacs	100
Conclusion	113
Index	119

Introduction

by Fredric Jameson

After the Soviet invasion of Czechoslovakia, which spelled a brutal end to Alexander Dubcek's "socialism with a human face," professional observers in France were astonished to find, contrary to all their expectations, that not the number of those defecting from the French Communist Party in disgust, but rather the number of new adherents to it, had increased! So it is that after all those momentous events—the disclosure of the Soviet camps, the invasion of South Korea, the revelations after the death of Stalin, the interventions, first in Hungary, and then, some fifteen years later, in Czechoslovakia—events confidently predicted to results in the demoralization of Communism as a political force and to the discrediting of Marxism as an influential mode of thinking, quite the opposite has taken place, and Marxism has found itself strengthened and rejuvenated by its liberation from the monolithic Soviet tradition. With the Chinese and Cuban Revolutions, the American New Left, the events of May 1968 in France, Marxism has emerged from the arthritis of Stalinism as a freshly creative and pluralistic school of thought and of action.

Indeed, we might do better to say that it has acquired its new philosophical vitality as though for the first time; and one of the principal signs of such vitality is the appearance of an increasing number of works which re-examine the history of Marxism itself from a genuinely Marxist point of view, and which make plain why this should be so, and why the most exciting questions about Marxist practice and theory have only just begun to be raised with all the philosophical subtlety and sophistication which they merit. Thus, even for the more limited and specific field of Marxist esthetics which concerns us here, such recent scholarship as that of Adolfo Sánchez Vásquez and Stefan Morawski, as well as the older pioneering studies of Marx's own esthetic views by George Lukacs and Mikhail Lifshitz, have begun to make clear the extent to which the development of Marxist theory after the death of Marx was crippled in all domains by the reformist practice of the great labor parties and the influence of non- or pre-Marxist schools of thought such as positivism or neo-Kantianism.[1]

---

[1] Adolfo Sánchez Vásquez, *Estética y Marxismo* (México, D.F., 1970), "Los problemas de la estética marxista," Vol. I, pp. 17–73; Morawski, "The Aesthetic Views of Marx and Engels," *Journal of Aesthetics and Art Criticism,* Vol. XXVIII, No. 3 (Spring, 1970), pp. 301–314; George Lukacs, "Einfuhrung in die aesthetischen Schriften von Marx und Engels," in *Probleme der Aesthetik* (Neuwied, 1969); Mikhail Lifshitz, *The Philosophy of Art of Karl Marx* (New York, 1938); and see, for related references, Lee Baxandall, *Marxism and Aesthetics: An Annotated Bibliography* (New York, 1968). This critique of late nineteenth-century Marxism was given its first, classic formulation in George Lukacs, *History and Class Consciousness* (Cambridge, Mass., 1971), and Karl Korsch, *Marx-*

Thus Marxist theory, in esthetics as elsewhere, was only incompletely born when the Russian Revolution drew it powerfully into the sphere of influence of a single country, a country with its own unique revolutionary development and requirements. The present work of Henri Arvon, which studies what (if we include the Communist Party writers of Western Europe) may be called the Soviet tradition of Marxist esthetics, dramatizes the difficult coexistence between art and revolution, the dilemmas of artistic practice and esthetic theory in societies in the throes of socialist construction or confronted with the intense political agitation of immediately prerevolutionary social situations. Yet such a history, with all its depressing pages, may serve to confirm in arresting fashion the claim that Marxism, as a living philosophy, has only just begun to develop in its own right.

So it is that many of the most characteristic objections to Marxism—and even more characteristically, to Marxist esthetics—turn out to have been leveled at straw men when they do not presuppose, and attribute to Marxism, positions on philosophical problems which have only begun to be worked out at the present day. Listen to Plekhanov himself, the father of the sometimes disastrously influential concept of the "social equivalent of art," defend himself against the frequently heard charge that Marxist criticism is an extrinsic criticism which has no interest in purely literary or formal values: "Philosophy," he tells us, "has not superseded esthetics, but has on the contrary paved the way for it in the

---

ism and Philosophy (New York, 1970), both of which appeared in 1923.

intention of supplying it with a more solid foundation. The same is true of the materialistic critique of esthetics. In its attempt to find the social equivalent of a given literary phenomenon, such a critique would be false to its own nature if it failed to comprehend that the task cannot be limited to the mere discovery of such an equivalent, and that sociology must not slam the door in the face of esthetics but rather fling it open wide. The second act of any consequent materialistic critique must therefore, just as for idealistic kinds, involve a judgment as to the esthetic value of the production in question. If the materialistic critic renounced such judgment on the grounds that he had already discovered the work's social equivalent, then that would only go to show that he had not grasped the real meaning of the philosophical position he claims to represent. The characteristics of the artistic production of a given period stand in the closest causal relationship to the social mentality expressed in it. The social mentality of an age is however always conditioned by that age's social relations. This is nowhere quite as evident as in the history of art and literature. The determination of the social equivalent of a given literary work would therefore remain incomplete, and consequently also inexact, if the critic abdicated any judgment as to its esthetic value. In other words, the first act of any materialistic critique does not only not make this second act superfluous, it positively presupposes the latter as its own necessary completion." [2]

[2] G. V. Plekhanov, "Introduction to *Za dvatsat let*," in *Sochinenia* (Moscow, 1924), Vol. XIV, p. 189; quoted in Viktor Žmegač, ed., *Marxistische Literaturkritik* (Bad Homburg, 1970), p. 11.

But it is one thing to show the groundlessness of many of the objections to a Marxist esthetics, and another to say positively what it is and how it functions. A Marxist esthetics—or a Marxist criticism—is called upon, it seems to me, to do four different kinds of things, or to solve four different kinds of problems. First of all, it can inquire into the general status of art and literature itself—this is to say that in practice such an esthetics will ask questions about the very beginnings of art in the evolution of human existence; and it will no doubt end up projecting some vision of the role art ought to play in a genuinely healthy society. Such an investigation I call genetic, in that it is primarily historical in character, at the same time that it seeks to solve the abstract questions (What is beauty? Is there a properly esthetic cognition? What is the function of art in human life and society?) with which the older philosophical domain of esthetics had always been concerned.

But a Marxist esthetic investigation can also ask quite different types of questions: it can for example seek to define the role which art ought to play in a *socialist* society, which is to say, at least in our own time, in a society seeking to construct socialism (and such is indeed the primary subject of the present work). Going even further, this kind of Marxist esthetic or criticism can seek to define the political function and the political tasks of art; and such concerns, it seems to me, imply a prescriptive kind of esthetic, one which encourages the artists and writers themselves to produce a particular type of art for a particular political purpose. Such prescription, while it seems to me perfectly legitimate, ought to speak with the authority of a political movement or a party, for it ought to be able to appeal to that part of the artist's mind and intelligence which longs to unite itself with some more fundamental collective being and practice. It is thus not the realm of the individual, isolated critic, except on the level of mere opinions on the subject.

The other two types of Marxist criticism are more "literary," in that they deal neither with the theory of art in general nor with engaged, political literature, but rather confront the existing literary works of the past and the present in an attempt to determine what ought to be the Marxist attitude toward such works which may be formalistic or nonpolitical when they are not downright conservative in their ideological orientation. Here it seems appropriate to distinguish between our critical study of works of the past and of other cultures, and the critical evaluations we make of contemporary writing and of the cultural production of the affluent, postindustrial society of American monopoly capitalism. The latter may be seen as part of that systematic enterprise of demystification and of tireless ideological analysis which is undoubtedly the most fundamental role which a Marxist criticism or journalism can fulfill for the public at large.

The former type of research—bearing on the history of literature—is no doubt more properly what is known as academic criticism and indeed finds its primary expression in teaching. We should think of this kind of scholarly research as a laboratory in which we attempt to determine the relationship between culture and cultural production, and the social and economic context in which such production takes place. It is the privileged domain of the theory of ideology and of the study of the relationship between what Marxism calls the superstructure and the base (or infrastructure). Such research is in reality intimately related to the kinds of committed and political judgments we make in the present; and it is quite different from the detached and antiquarian attitude toward a dead past which is encouraged by bourgeois historiography.

I have often thought, indeed, that Schleiermacher's notion of a "hermeneutic circle" offered the most convenient symbol for the way in which the present is renewed by such contact with the past. Schleiermacher had in mind the circular process of understanding itself, in which we read the parts in the light of the whole, but cannot presumably know the whole at all until we have read all the parts; in which we understand the individual words against the background of a projected sentence which will, however, not be complete until we have finished reading each of the words one by one. The same circle (or spiral) holds, it seems to me, for our comprehension of the past. No doubt, the degree to which we can have a vivid sense of the great struggles of the past, and of the social conflict from which the greatest works have emerged, is directly proportionate to our own personal experience of just such conflicts in the present. So the political struggles of the last decade have renewed our understanding of the past as well, and caused us to see in a new light many of those masterpieces of the past which for an apolitical generation had been felt as mere art objects or formal constructions.

Yet there is another sense in which the present is too complicated for us to grasp, for we are inside it, and it is, moreover, new and different and not yet fully charted by theories developed for earlier situations. What is, for example, class struggle in the United States today? And, indeed, which are the classes themselves and what kind of consciousness do they possess, how do they relate to each other in the daily life of our society? We would be most embarrassed to be confronted with such ultimate theoretical questions, which are indeed the most urgent problem of Marxist research in the United States today. Thus it turns out that it is precisely from the past that we begin to learn what class struggle is, and the devious relationship to it which the consciousness and the culture of man have entertained. The past, simpler than the present, offers a kind of model from which we can begin to learn the realities of history itself, and from its study, we return to the present, not with the answers, but with the questions clarified in our minds for the first time. What is satisfying about the Marxist vision of history is that for it the events of man's reign on earth tell a single story and share a common theme, encourage us in a solidarity with the works and deeds of vanished or alien cultures and generations.

One can, however, well understand the exasperation of the nondialectical reader with a fourfold esthetic scheme of this kind, which appears to make the most contradictory and mutually exclusive options all possible simultaneously, and to amount to a way of being right no matter how things ultimately turn out. It is, however, the very essence of dialectical thinking that we do not have to do with some static logical system, in which abstract positions can be worked out in the void with some kind of finality, but rather with a doctrine of the concrete, for which each problem must be re-evaluated in the light of the unique historical situation in which it arises. Thus we may well have a passionate appreciation for the struggle to create a genuinely political art in an immediately prerevolutionary situation (such as that of the Germany of the nineteen-twenties), without feeling that the intransigent and overtly political standards of such an art are particularly applicable to the state of consciousness and culture in the United States today, where more sophisticated diagnostic techniques are necessary to win over an imperfectly committed intelligentsia and a brainwashed middle and lower-middle class. From such a vantage point, both Brecht and Lukacs (whose debate on this subject is described at length in Chapter 7 of the present work) can be said to be right, and to say so is not to confirm a double standard but rather to reassert the primacy of situational thinking in both theory and practice.

In a more general way, however, I often feel that many of the reproaches addressed to a Marxist esthetics more properly reflect a kind of perplexity before the problems of historicity itself, and, in particular, of our relationship to the past. So the dilemma which Professor Arvon evokes at the very opening of his book—the apparent contradiction between the "eternal" or atemporal value of a great work of the past, and the historical roots it must evidently have had in a wholly different social world from our own—is not in fact a peculiarly Marxist one, but one shared by all historical thinking. It is essentially an esthetic version of that more general problem of the relativization of the past which tormented the theoreticians of German historicism at the turn of the century; and, if anything, Marxism distinguishes itself from those positions by furnishing the elements of a solution to it.

Such a solution, it seems to me, would have to take into account three essential features of the problem—first of all, our attitude toward other stages of socioeconomic development and other cultures (and it is with this that Marx himself is concerned in the famous passage of Greek art which Professor Arvon quotes); then, the whole matter of what artistic "greatness" may be said to amount to in a Marxist context; and finally, the apparent difficulty of reconciling purely esthetic appreciation, or the apprehension of what the estheticians would call "beauty," and those harsh and negative judgments which a Marxist critic is called upon to make on ideological manifestations of all kinds.

So far as Marx's own question is concerned ("the difficulty we are confronted with is not that of understanding how Greek art and epic poetry are associated with certain forms of social development. The difficulty is that they still give us esthetic pleasure and are in certain respects regarded as a standard and unattainable ideal" [3]), the solution is already implicit in that extended comparison between the ages of history and the growth of an individual with which Marx's fragmentary text breaks off. Precapitalist art, and particularly the art of ancient Greece, reflects a world in which the division of labor has not yet taken place, in which the market and commodity system has not yet

[3] Karl Marx, *A Contribution to the Critique of Political Economy* (New York, 1970), Introduction of 1857, p. 217.

made an abstraction of human experience. So it is scarcely surprising that out of the alienating structures of nineteenth- and twentieth-century capitalism we should look back with a (not necessarily unrevolutionary) nostalgia at such moments in which life, and form, are still relatively whole, and which seem at the same time to afford a glimpse into the nature of some future nonalienated existence as well.

This does not mean that such earlier precapitalist societies were in any sense utopias; on the contrary they knew the most brutal forms of physical oppression, and the art of ancient Greece in particular developed out of the leisure afforded by a slave system. Yet such oppression and such violence were individual and personal and wore human forms; they were visible to the naked eye, and could be reckoned back into man's experience of the social totality, whereas the qualitatively new violence characteristic of capitalism is an abstract and institutionalized kind, which can no longer be grasped in terms of our everyday, existential experience, and which thus increasingly tends to escape expression through artistic means. So what is surprising in the long run is not so much that we are attracted to the art of precapitalist societies and cultures, but indeed that capitalism itself should have produced any art worthy of the name in the first place.

The question of esthetic value or greatness is the principal weapon in the polemic conventionally waged against sociological approaches to literature in general and Marxist esthetics in particular. Characteristically, it involves questions like this: if you insist on looking at works of literature as reflections of their social context, how are you going to distinguish between a great writer like Racine and a mediocre contemporary like Pradon, since presumably they share the same context? It is certain, indeed, that if we insist on understanding the relationship of the individual to his social background according to the static model of traditional logic, then such a question is unanswerable, and Racine and Pradon—members of the same abstract class or set, individual embodiments of the abstract genus "Versailles esthete," or ideological court spokesman—end up being as indistinguishable from each other as the individual fruits which make up the category "apple." (As for the notion of the deterministic influence of the milieu, it is a positivistic, rather than a dialectical and Marxist, concept, and there does not seem to be much point in refuting a doctrine which no one has ever been able to argue clearly in the first place.)

Such a static model is, however, not at all implicit in Marxist theory, and as an example of different and more satisfying approaches, we may refer to Sartre's recent descriptions of the way in which each individual *reinvents*, in his own unique style and fashion, that social class of which he is a member. Such a theoretical solution makes a far more adequate place for individual difference and individual creativity, at the same time that it reminds us to include, within our concept of the social context, the formative experience of childhood itself: for Sartre, indeed, childhood is a *mediation* between individual existence and the structures of the social group; it is the moment in which the individual is socially formed, formed, however, through the process of forming himself within the social microcosm of the family.[4]

Still, some of the force of this particular objection derives from our sense of personal and individual *difference,* a legacy of the Romantic movement which leads us to believe that genius, in art as elsewhere, is that which is unique and pre-eminently uncharacteristic. To have tirelessly denounced this misconception was the merit of Lucien Goldmann, who taught us that it is precisely the greatest works of art which are the *most* representative of their era: "The writer of genius seems to us to be the one who realizes a synthesis, whose work is *at one and the same time* the most immediate and the most philosophically aware, for *his sensibility coincides with the ensemble of the process and of the historical evolution;* the genius is he who, in order to speak about his own most concrete and immediate problems, implicitly raises the most general problems of his age and of his culture, and for whom, inversely, all the *essential problems* of his time are not mere intellectualizations or abstract convictions but realities which are manifested in living and immediate fashion in his very feelings and intuitions." [5]

This means, in the present context, that there is in reality no contradiction between the "eternal" value of a work and its profound historicity; on the contrary, the two are for Marxism one, and the esthetic greatness of a work is directly proportionate to its historical representativeness, to the completeness with which it dramatizes all the contradictions of its age. (This is perhaps the moment to add that a Marxist

[4] J.-P. Sartre, *Search for a Method,* trans. Hazel E. Barnes (New York, 1968), esp. pp. 57–65.
[5] Lucien Goldmann, *Recherches dialectiques* (Paris, 1959), p. 60.

esthetic is by no means indissolubly wedded to a preference for realism as against artistic stylization, but rather that under certain circumstances and in certain historical situations—such as our own—a stylized and abstract art, such as that of Gombrowicz or of Robbe-Grillet, may in fact in the long run prove more representative and more profoundly historical in character.)

Ultimately, however, the problem of esthetic "greatness" is a false one, for it involves a kind of illicit and a priori reconstruction of the esthetic experience itself. In reality we never are called on to choose between Racine and Pradon, and what comes first is the lived experience of the literary work itself, the shock of its esthetic effect or indeed the boredom which lets the book droop from our hands. Literary theory and literary criticism are thus attempts to account for this concrete experience *after the fact:* they can never function a priori or predictively, not even in such an artificial and hypothetical confrontation as that between Racine and Pradon. We would thus be tempted to reverse the procedures described by Plekhanov in the passage quoted above, and to claim that if a Marxist criticism is called upon to complete the purely formal and "esthetic" experience of the work, this is because it is only through such a social and historical regrounding that the formal experience can reach its greatest intensity in the first place.

The final aspect of the problem of our relationship to the art of the past is that of the critique of ideology; and it is customarily assumed that the critical judgments which we may make on a writer in this respect imply related strictures on his artistic worth. Thus the naive reader—even one willing to experiment with Marxist thought-modes—expects the ideological critique of a work to supply him with hard and fast value judgments as well. For him the conclusion that, say, George Eliot was a reactionary, is tantamount to an admission that she was a bad writer as well; if on the contrary he admires her art, then presumably he feels obliged to justify his admiration by uncovering "progressive" aspects of her work.

But what if our relationship to the past, and to its acts and works, were far more complicated than this? Already Lukacs, in a *locus classicus* of Marxist theory, took it upon himself to convince vulgar Marxists that an adequate view of Balzac involved a coming to terms with his reactionary social and political views as well as an appreciation of his realistic narrative practice.[6] Indeed, we probably have to go even further than Lukacs did and see these two antithetical aspects of Balzac's work as mutually interdependent and, in his case, inconceivable the one without the other. For the counterrevolutionary attitudes of Balzac's generation, as well as of the preceding one, that of Edmund Burke, were born of a fear of Jacobinism, no doubt, and of that social upheaval which threatened to sweep away the last vestiges of the old feudal institutions; yet inasmuch as those changes themselves amounted to the coming to power of the bourgeoisie and the installation of the capitalist system, Romantic reaction is itself anticapitalistic, and constitutes a negative and critical standpoint from which to observe the new world of the market system in all its unlovely detail. As a

[6] George Lukacs, "The Peasants," in *Studies in European Realism* (London, 1950), pp. 21–46.

critique of capitalism, then, if not as a solution to the social and economic problems it brought with it, Romantic reaction anticipates the diagnosis of Marxism itself, so that it is not at all surprising that Marx should have found in the novels of Balzac a kindred view of the world.

A dialectical view of history strengthens us in the conclusion that our relationship to the past can never be that of univocal moral judgments but always involves what amount to structurally determinate ambiguities, historical mixed feelings. I have tried to articulate elsewhere [7] the ways in which the kinds of judgments we make on works of art—as progressive or reactionary, as ideological document or formal artifact—vary themselves in function of our practical distance from the past and from history: a really complete act of historical apprehension would indeed involve all of these apparently contradictory judgments in turn, if not simultaneously, for the works of the art of the past are always all these things at once, class apologia just as much as sheer formal invention, and the realities they express involve both positive and negative impulses together, both "progressive" and "reactionary" elements.

To answer such preliminary objections to a Marxist esthetics is also to suggest ways in which such an esthetics, and the literary criticism based on it, may be expected to evolve in the future. Yet for dialectical philosophy, the fortunes of a theory or concept are inseparable from the history of its previous development; and in the present case it is abundantly clear that such an evolution does not take place in a void, but against the background of the concrete diffi-

[7] See my *Marxism and Form* (Princeton, 1971), pp. 375–390.

culties with which Marxist esthetics have met in the course of real history.

It is, of course, a story which has been told many times, particularly with reference to Soviet Marxism; but it has always been told by Sovietologists or by Slavicists for whom Marxism was itself by definition something to be understood from the outside—as dogma, propaganda, or the vicissitudes of the party line. Now for the first time in English, Professor Arvon's book provides a history of the development of Marxist esthetics from a point of view sympathetic to the basic aims of Marxism itself. He reminds us of the cultural and intellectual pluralism of the early Soviet period, and shows that alongside the other modernist currents, many of them prerevolutionary, there existed a specifically revolutionary modernism of more than antiquarian interest for us today.

Professor Arvon's account of the Brecht-Lukacs debate, moreover, demonstrates that even under Stalinism esthetic issues of the greatest significance were still to be raised and debated among Communists; and his treatment of this grim period puts it in proper historical perspective while disengaging what is for Professor Arvon the central problem of any Marxist esthetic.

For even if we have today come to understand that the revolutionary and postrevolutionary experience of the Soviet Union is only one of the historic forms which the creation of a socialist society can take, the newer revolutions will continue to face, in their own specific social and cultural contexts, the problem of the relationship of artistic production to the construction of socialism. The newer revolutions indeed have repeatedly dramatized for us that critical moment in which a prerevolutionary, essentially negative and critical art is called upon to give way to one which might be expected to contribute in some positive fashion to the revolutionary effort of a whole society.

In our own nonrevolutionary situation, such an alternative may seem of only theoretical interest. Professor Arvon's history reminds us, however, that the dilemma of the status of art under revolutionary conditions is profoundly symptomatic of the fate of revolutionary consciousness in general, or of what is called today "cultural revolution." For a middle-class state, art is a luxury, when it is not an investment; for a socialist one, it is the indispensable sign of the reintegration of a fragmented, alienated existence.

Marxist Esthetics

1

Marxism and Art

"What makes art an eternal value despite its historicity?" This question, posed in such trenchant and inescapable terms by Karl Marx in his introduction to *The Critique of Political Economy* (1859), immediately reveals the dilemma with which any esthetic theory that deliberately shuts itself up within the narrow confines of an exclusively temporal perspective must wrestle. To maintain that art is by nature historically determined is tantamount not only to linking all artistic phenomena more or less closely to a certain specific situation, but above all to refusing, a priori, to consider art as having any permanent meaning or, even more importantly, any absolute value. Idealistic esthetics encounters little difficulty in discovering the eternal laws of the beautiful and of esthetic value in the shimmering mirrors of artistic phenomena, since by taking certain metaphysical statements as its point of departure it immediately turns its back on the arbitrary nature of contingency. An esthetic, on the other hand, that recognizes only historical evolution as a science would appear to have no chance of becoming a normative discipline.

But how can esthetics avoid referring to history, when it is obvious that it is possible, and even necessary, to interpret the work of art as the product of historical factors that both recur and change unceasingly? It is these dimensions of interpretability, subject to constant variation, that inevitably make it necessary to place art back within this field of fundamental meanings uniquely characteristic of each period. Hypostasized esthetics, by contrast, obliges the contemplator to envisage the beautiful only in its intemporal aspect, and thus such an esthetic in the end becomes gratuitous speculation, useless and beside the point.

By requiring that dialectics bring about the difficult, if not impossible, conjoining of the temporal and the eternal, of historical value and absolute value, Marxist esthetics submits it to the supreme and crucial test. That is why the "science of art" seems destined to occupy a privileged place within Marxist doctrine. Gorky declared that "esthetics [is] the ethics of the future." Roger Garaudy, the author of *Réalisme sans rivages* [Boundless Realism], unhesitatingly states that "the conception of esthetics is the touchstone of the interpretation of Marxism." But it is above all George Lukacs, who has been rightly called "the Marx of esthetics," who has deliberately chosen the realm of esthetics as the focal point of his effort to revise Marxist dialectics and broaden its scope so as to enable it to deal with present-day problems.

Marxist esthetics remains all the more open to a total and ever-changing application of dialectics in that it is one of the rare branches of Marxist doctrine not to have been crushed and smothered beneath the weight of rigid dogma established once and for all and drummed into its proponents by an almost ritualistic recitation of magic formulas. Thought and felt to be at times a tool for coercively inculcating doctrine, at times the free expression of fervent revolutionary hope, at times an evidence of reassuring continuity, at times a sudden break, taking on by turn a revolutionary form that causes its conservative content to be overlooked and a content that is all the more revolutionary in that its form remains traditional, art posed problems for Marx and his successors when they attempted to incorporate it within their overall view of social and historical phenomena. They tried, certainly, to deal with these problems, but they were never able definitely to solve them. The prisoners either of their personal tastes or of the imperatives of political action, they never succeeded, despite efforts that at times were desperate, in penetrating beyond the outer boundaries of an esthetic.

This was true of Karl Marx in particular. Though as a theoretician he was first drawn to philosophy and later to politics and economics, Marx nonetheless was interested in esthetic questions all his life. During his philosophical period, he planned to publish studies of religious art and Romanticism, and at one point he wanted to write a book on Balzac once he finished *Capital*. For lack of time, these projects were never carried out. His literary criticism, in the strict sense of the word, is thus limited to two occasional pieces. *The Holy Family* contains a criticism of the commentary, written by a young Hegelian named Szeliga, on Eugène Sue's *Mysteries of Paris*. The other document is his famous correspondence with Ferdinand Lassalle concerning the latter's play *Franz von Sickingen*. The first of these two pieces of criticism is social in nature rather than literary. Eugène Sue, who at the time was enjoying, not only in France but also in Germany, a popularity quite disproportionate to the literary value of his works, is accused by Marx of launching an attack on social injustice that is purely illusory, since Sue does not attack capitalist society itself. The critique of Lassalle's play, on the other hand, is not confined to criteria exterior to the work. It thus provides the first broad outlines of a specifically Marxist esthetic.

Another factor contributing to the complexity of Marx's attitude toward art, the ambivalence, if not the contradiction, between the bourgeois way of life he clung to even amid extreme poverty, and the antibourgeois way of thinking he adopted in his early years and never abandoned, is nowhere as clearly evident as in his remarks on works of literature. He especially appreciates the style of writers in the great tradition, and thus greatly admires Aeschylus, Shakespeare, Goethe, Scott, and Balzac. His literary judgments of contemporary writers, on the other hand, are determined by their political attitudes: he thus is partial to Freiligrath and Georg Herwegh, who are minor poets but champions of freedom.

We therefore find a certain inconsistency in the scattered comments of Karl Marx and Friedrich Engels on art and especially on literature. But in most cases this inconsistency is more apparent than real.

Like Marxist doctrine as a whole, Marxist esthetics can be understood only in the light of the Hegelian philosophy from which it stemmed. Having taken Hegelian dialectics as their point of departure and "stood it on its head," as they put it, Marx and Engels inevitably view art and literature from a Hegelian perspective, whether adopting that perspective as their own or standing somewhat apart from it or squarely opposing it.

Marx and Engels have a particularly high regard for the novelists of the bourgeois period, Fielding, Balzac, and the Russian realists, and are fond of pointing out how critical these writers are of the social and political world in which they live. Their preference for these writers is based on Hegelian esthetic principles. Faithful to the esthetics of the Age of Enlightenment as developed by Wieland and Goethe, Hegel regarded the novel as the bourgeois form of the epic. Whereas the epic reflects the whole of life, in his view, the novel was born of "the conflict between the poetry of the heart and the prose of the situation that is its opposite, losing itself in the exterior and the contingent." In the epic, the subjective is raised to the level of the typical; in the novel, which corresponds to an era in which the Self and the world are divided, the relations between the subjective and the typical become problematical.

It is precisely because Hegel's esthetic, through its analysis of details, provides a picture of the process of evolution of human societies that it serves as a propaedeutic to Marxist esthetics. Thus the relationship between social forms and artistic forms that Hegel establishes in his study of Dutch painting in the seventeenth century strikes the Russian Marxist G. V. Plekhanov as particularly revealing. Hegel points out that the miracle of Dutch painting is a perfect reflection of the physical surroundings and the daily life of Dutchmen: "The joy the Dutch took in life, even in its most ordinary and trivial aspects," Hegel writes, "stemmed from the fact that they were forced to conquer, at the price of a very difficult struggle and painful efforts, what nature offers other people without a struggle and without effort. . . . The Dutch created most of the soil on which they live with their own hands; they were obliged to defend it ceaselessly against the assaults of the sea. This civic pride, this spirit of enterprise, this joyous and exuberant consciousness of self they owe entirely to their own efforts, to their own activity, and that is what constitutes the general content of their paintings."

The classic tastes of Marx and Engels, which if not totally inconsistent with their political and philosophical convictions are at least peripheral to them, are difficult to reconcile with the famous Hegelian thesis concerning the mortality or rather the death of art. In Hegel's absolute idealism, there are three well-known stages in the march of the Spirit toward the Absolute: art, which is "the revelation of the Absolute in its intuitive form, pure appearance, an ideality that shines through the real while at the same time remaining ideality over and against the objectivity of the human ethical world"; religion; and philosophy. Art reaches its pinnacle in ancient Greece, religion flowers in Christianity, and philosophy eventually raises both art and religion to the level of knowledge of the Absolute, that is to say, absolute knowledge. In this progression of Spirit through three stages, art is thus merely a temporary and incomplete phase, which is limited in time. The moment that humanity attains the supreme stage of philosophy through Hegelian thought, art is relegated to the rank of an outmoded investigation of reality that has been superseded. For the modern era, past culture is merely an imaginary museum, so to speak. "From the point of view of its ultimate end, at least," Hegel writes in the introduction to his *Esthetics,* "[art] for us is a thing of the past. It has lost its truth and its life for us. It invites us to engage in a philosophical reflection whose aim is not to bring about its rebirth, but to acquire a rigorous knowledge of its essence." Like Plato, who banishes Homer from the ideal Republic, though first wreathing him in flowers because he greatly respects his poetry, Hegel rejects the art of his time and considers philosophy the only true reflection of reality.

Marx in turn also regards artistic expression as having reached its pinnacle and its purest form in Greek art. In his eyes the Greek miracle is more or less an inaccessible peak of human achievement. But because he judges art not only from the point of view of the overall evolution of humanity, but also in its dialectical relations with the various social and economic stages through which mankind has passed in the course of this evolution, Marx at this point counters Hegel's arguments. Whereas the latter speaks of the harmony of the Greeks as that of a "milieu which nonetheless, like life in general, is only a transitory phase, even though in this transitory phase it reaches the very apogee of beauty," Marx in his introduction to *The Critique of Political Economy* stresses the apparent contradiction between the specific historical factors determining the nature of Greek art which on the one hand ought to confine our interpretation and our appreciation of it within certain limits, and the permanent attraction that it holds for mankind despite all historical changes on the other.

Greek art is very closely linked, certainly, to Greek social conditions. "Is Achilles possible in an age of firearms, or the *Iliad* in general in an age of printed books?" There is nothing more natural and less surprising than this parallelism between social forms and artistic forms. But Marx immediately poses the crucial question, which is not sociological or ideological in nature, but purely and simply esthetic: "It is not difficult to grasp the fact that Greek art and the Greek epic are linked to certain social forms. What is difficult to understand is why they also offer us esthetic pleasure and in a certain sense appear to be norms and matchless models."

It is precisely because certain important forms of art can flower only in a very early or very primitive phase of artistic evolution that we remain receptive to the meaning of Greek art; since it is an expression of the magic of humanity's childhood, it brings back memories of our own childhood. "The attraction that their art has for us," Marx writes, "is not in contradiction with the feeble development of the society in which it evolved. On the contrary, it is the result of it. It is indissolubly linked with the fact that the rudimentary state of society in which this art was born, the only one in which it could be born, will never again recur."

In a doctrine which establishes the strictest ties between subjective phenomena and social relationships, this is how Marx has dealt with the Greek miracle, which is proof of the fact that the general level of development of society and that of art may not always go absolutely hand in hand. In point of fact, Marx's customary argument that their evolution is parallel takes a rather unusual turn here; in this particular instance, the requirements of historical materialism can be met only by maintaining that the case of Greek art is exceptional and by rejecting this parallelism as an explanation of the esthetic pleasure that results from that art. When Marx discusses the pleasure that the adult feels when he recalls his childhood, do we not find a quite close resemblance to the theme of our nostalgia for our lost innocence, most brilliantly described by Schiller in his *On Naive and Sentimental Poetry?*

It is in their conception of tragedy and the hero that Marx and Engels most clearly part company with Hegelian esthetics. Hegel's ideas concerning the hero went through two successive stages. In his earlier writings, the hero was a figure belonging to the very early days of antiquity when men still enjoyed absolute freedom of action. In his later writings, the hero is regarded as the man whom historical evolution outstrips, yet who desperately attempts to resist the march of history by defending the old order to which he belongs against the principles of the new society that rejects him. Thus Hegel praises Goethe for having chosen Götz von Berlichingen, a knight rebelling against an era in which he has no place, as the hero of one of his tragedies.

Marx's and Engels' criticism of Lassalle's play *Franz von Sickingen* affords them an opportunity to deal with the concept of the hero and adapt it to the needs of an esthetic aimed at fulfilling historical necesities of the moment. This was, in fact, what Lassalle had been attempting to do by writing his play. The esthetician Friedrich Theodor Vischer, who had been deeply influenced by Hegelian ideas and whose *Esthetics* was largely inspired by them, had written an article entitled "Shakespeare and his Relation to German

Poetry" in which he argued that all dramatic works must have a historical content, as Hegel had also demanded. It was precisely this predominance of history over individual wills that Lassalle had endeavored to illustrate. By contrast to Schiller's subjective drama, Lassalle's play is not centered on the personal destiny of the hero, but on the pressure exercised on him by the objective spirit, that is to say by the class struggle in which he is caught up, willy-nilly, and by the ideological struggle in which he is forced to take sides. In Lassalle's view, the drama of Franz von Sickingen is not an isolated historical event; it foreshadows, anticipates, and explains the failure of the Revolution of 1848.

But far from viewing Lassalle's play as an exemplary tragedy of Revolution and the workings of the all-powerful objective spirit, Marx and Engels discovered in it a subjective element that the author had done his best to eliminate but had merely contrived to conceal beneath clumsy and artificial draperies. The real subject of Lassalle's drama is the action of an individual who is seeking to be "crafty about great events," who believes that he can shape history through his own cynically realistic policy alone. Taking no account whatsoever of the objective historical facts, Franz von Sickingen aspires to the imperial crown; he betrays his nation and his friends, and through this betrayal betrays himself. Thus the tragedy that Lassalle has done his best to place within a social framework in the final analysis is nothing more than a simple psychological and moral problem. Though Lassalle has taken Shakespeare's historical plays as his model in *Franz von Sickingen,* what his drama resembles far more is the pathos-laden declamations of Schiller. There is another factor that makes the failure of the play all the more inevitable in Marx's view: though Lassalle has adopted the ethical interpretation of history, he has failed to bring about the reconciliation of the subjective and the objective implicit in Schiller's and Hegel's tragic idealism. Since the tragic dialectic is shifted to the course of history itself on the one hand and to Sickingen's individual action on the other, it ends in a hopeless blind alley. Lassalle's play would lead us to believe that the defeat of any social movement is inevitable because Revolution itself is fatally flawed.

In any event, Sickingen's end cannot be regarded as tragic; it is willed by history and determined by it. A thieving knight-errant and a holdover from the feudal era, Sickingen is doomed to disappear the moment a bourgeois economy develops. It is therefore not correct to see him as the very epitome of the hero. The same is true of Götz von Berlichingen, for unlike Hegel, Marx does not consider him to be a hero at all, but rather a "miserable man," a representative of chivalry, a class which historical evolution has caused to fall by the wayside—a class destined to disappear. Marx's disapproval of Götz as a figure in history does not entail a condemnation of Goethe's play about him however. On the contrary; Marx finds in Goethe's work the dynamic complexity of the march of history whose absence he deplores in Lassalle's play, which is nothing more than an abstract illustration of progress.

The true hero, according to Marx and Engels, is not out of step with his own time. He does not exhaust himself in fruitless rear-guard skirmishes; he is ahead of his time; he accelerates history rather than endeavoring to halt its onward march. The hero must be sought for among the revolutionaries of the past, among the plebes in revolt or the peasants of Thomas Münzer. His defeat is never final, the heroic dream that spurs him on is only the first faint glimpse of a future that will dawn sooner or later.

However limited the esthetic reflections Marx and Engels put forward in the few pages they devote to art and literature, they nonetheless unveil a threefold perspective, without our being able to discern a priori which of the three aspects involved is paramount, for at times they view art as totally dependent on the social situation, at times as completely autonomous, and at times as an instrument of political action. Consequently, art for the successors of Marx and Engels is an area that is only vaguely and imperfectly outlined, and personal preferences and particular artistic sensibilities will play a decisive role in their esthetic theories.

For G. V. Plekhanov (1856–1918), the Russian translator of the *Communist Manifesto* and Lenin's mentor before becoming his adversary, "literature and art are the mirror of social life." Since artistic works are phenomena or products stemming from social relations, it is possible to "translate works of art from the language of art into that of sociology." A knowledge of the artist or the author himself is therefore not as essential for the complete understanding of the work of art or literature as is the social psychology he necessarily shares with his contemporaries. "Every literary work is the expression of its time," Plekhanov states in his polemic against Gustave Lanson, the champion of literary individuality. "Its content and its form are determined by the tastes, the habits, and the tendencies of that time, and the greater the writer, the more strict and more obvious this dependence that subordinates the nature of his work to the nature of his time, or, in other words, the less one finds in his works that 'residue' that might be called personal. The hallmark, the 'superior originality' (the reader will recall this expression of Lanson's) of a great man lies in the fact that in his own field of endeavor he has been able to express the aspirations and the social or spiritual needs of his age before others, better than others, and more completely than others. All other particularities disappear in the face of this one particularity that constitutes his 'historic individuality,' as stars disappear in the light of day. And such individuality may very well become the object of a precise scientific analysis."

The method that logically follows from these considerations is the total rejection of individual creative genius and the absolute priority of scientific facts; Plekhanov himself carefully indicates the successive steps leading from economics to art in esthetic analysis of this sort: "the status of productive forces, the economic relations conditioned by these forces, the social and political system built upon this economic foundation, the psychology of social man determined in part directly by economics, in part by the social and political system built upon this economic substructure, diverse ideologies reflecting this psychology."

The distinction Plekhanov makes between esthetic judgment strictly speaking and the utilitarian purpose of art would seem to correspond to Marx's careful distinction between esthetic appreciation and the ultimate purpose of art.

There is one fundamental difference however. For Plekhanov, esthetic judgment belongs to the realm of pure theory, whereas Marx makes it a particular form of practical, everyday appreciation. Thus the strict separation between esthetic pleasure and the eminently social role of art in Plekhanov's esthetic is not so much the result of an overly rigid application of historical and dialectical materialism as the result of the influence that the radical Russian critics of the 1860's, in particular V. G. Belinsky and N. G. Chernyshevsky, his acknowledged mentors, had on him, just as to a greater or lesser degree they influenced all the Russian Marxists. Art that regards the providing of esthetic pleasure as its principal goal is considered to be an aristocratic luxury and therefore condemned absolutely; art can redeem itself only by serving the people.

Despite this uncompromisingly sociological approach, Plekhanov nonetheless refuses to put art and literature in the service of party politics: "Esthetics has no orders whatsoever to give art; it does not say to it: you must follow such and such rules or examples. It modestly limits itself to observing how the various rules and models that have prevailed in various periods of history have come to be the standard . . . it finds everything acceptable in its own particular time . . . it is as objective as physics."

In his article "Organization and Party Literature," written in 1905, V. I. Lenin condemns outright any literary activity that does not further the efforts of the Party. Literature in his view fulfills a social function; it serves as a guide for revolutionary action by arousing, maintaining, and enhancing people's awareness of social realities, and it profits in turn from the lessons taught by revolutionary struggle. Viewed in this light, Marxist esthetics becomes a sort of technology of indoctrination and propaganda; its purpose is to discover how art and literature can be used to control and shape political attitudes. Lenin's anathema against politically uncommitted literature is famous: "Let us rid ourselves of men of letters without a party! Let us rid ourselves of literary supermen! The cause of literature must become a part of the general cause of the proletariat, a little cog in the great unified mechanism of social democracy set in motion by the entire revolutionary working-class avant-garde as a whole. Literary activity must become a basic element in the work of the organized, disciplined, and united social-democratic party."

It is this particularly explicit and unusually harsh text of Lenin's that was taken as gospel during the dark era of Zhdanovism. The *partignost* (Party spirit) that Lenin wanted to make the motivating force of all cultural life was thereupon made compulsory for artists and above all for writers, whose role was reduced to that of simple cogs in the vast Soviet machine. The only task assigned them was the servile exemplification and glorification of Party decisions.

It is important, however, not to overestimate the actual significance of Lenin's article. N. Krupskaya, his wife and closest collaborator, stated in a letter that the sole purpose of this text was to lay down guidelines for the press and Party publications; it did not concern creative works of literature at all. Moreover, Lenin constantly contrasted the mere show of freedom enjoyed by bourgeois writers and artists, who were more or less forced to prostitute themselves in a world dominated by money and riddled with corruption, with the genuine freedom offered those engaged in cultural activities by Socialist society. In other instances he preaches the need for as liberal an attitude as possible with regard to literary creation. "There is no doubt," he writes in his book *Concerning Art and Culture,* "that it is literary activity that can least tolerate a mechanical egalitarianism, a domination of the minority by the majority. There is no doubt that in this domain the assurance of a rather large field of action for thought and imagination, for form and content is absolutely necessary."

"It is precisely because Marxism enables man to discover the laws of social evolution and restores man's creative work, which determines this evolution, to its proper place that Socialism is the system most likely to safeguard man's cultural heritage. The superiority of Marxism lies in its ability to separate the wheat from the tares in the realm of culture, and true art and literature from idealist and mechanistic deviations due to the harmful influences of capitalism. Marxism," Lenin declares, "in no way rejects the most precious achievements of the bourgeois era."

In two articles on Tolstoy, "Tolstoy as a Mirror of the Russian Revolution," written in Geneva in 1908, and "Tolstoy and His Time," written in Saint Petersburg in 1911, Lenin stresses the fact that the work of literature is not simply a blind reflection of reality, but rather a mirror of it, that is to say, a work possessed of all the ambiguity of the reality that it depicts, and therefore it is the militant exegete who must fulfill the task of disclosing the ideology hidden within it. Thus behind Tolstoy's "false consciousness" Lenin detects the "social equivalent" of the Russian peasantry in the latter's historical frescoes; Tolstoy has managed to give his contingent writings the dimensions of historical necessity. His works are an implicit expression of the violent opposition to capitalism in its initial stages and to the driving of the rural masses from the land, and thus are a precise description of the particular features of middle-class and peasant life making for revolution in Russia.

Leon Trotsky grants literature almost total freedom. In his *Literature and Revolution,* published in 1924, he expresses no misgivings whatsoever about allowing the creative vitality of the Revolution to extend itself in the most unexpected and ostensibly the least "proletarian" directions. He himself is most enthusiastic about the many Futurist experiments and the new architectural style launched by the Bauhaus movement led by the German Walter Gropius. He dreams of a strictly functional urban art, of an art that will go hand in hand with industrial progress and humanize it. He is an outspoken adversary of "proletarian literature," for esthetic reasons firstly, "inasmuch as art for the proletariat must not be an art of an inferior quality," and for political reasons secondly, since in his view the dictatorship of the proletariat is simply a transitional stage.

Trotsky therefore does his utmost to preserve total creative freedom, with regard to both form and content, from the tyranny of dogmatic pronouncements; this freedom is not meant to function in a void, however, for it must be based on a Marxist interpretation of the esthetic fabric whose warp is social reality and whose woof is its many different cultural expressions. "Our Marxist conception of the objective dependence of art on society and its social usefulness when applied in the area of politics," he declares in *Literature and Revolution,* "does not in any way imply an effort to control art through decrees and prescriptions. It is not true that in our society we regard only art whose theme is the worker as new and revolutionary, and the belief that we force poets, willy-nilly, to write about nothing but factory chimneys or a revolt against capitalism is absurd."

"It is quite true that a work of art should never be judged, accepted, or rejected on the basis of Marxist principles. The products of artistic creation must be evaluated first and foremost on the basis of their own laws, that is to say the laws of art. But only Marxism is capable of explaining why and how a certain orientation of art came about at a certain period, that is to say the origin and the reason for such an orientation and not some other," he writes.

The fundamental underlying ambiguity of Marxist esthetics, which appears at times to be merely a method of explanation and at other times to be a normative doctrine setting down hard and fast rules, has an important effect on the applicability of this esthetics in various realms of the cultural universe. All avenues are open to it when its sole purpose is to examine the work of art in the light of historical materialism. Thus Marx seeks to explain the Greek miracle even though he confesses that it greatly perplexes him. But when Marxist esthetics turns into a vast program of indoctrination and political education, artistic creation, strictly speaking, the intellectual import of which is always difficult and often impossible to determine, inevitably becomes of secondary importance as compared to literature, whose means of expression can easily be dealt with in conceptual terms.

The difficulties encountered by Marxist esthetics when it attempts to deal with music are very revealing in this regard. The irrational nature of music led Kant to place it at the bottom of the hierarchy of the arts, while for the same reason Schopenhauer placed it at the top. Marxism has gone to impossible lengths in its endeavor to enroll it in the service of a praxis bearing a dialectical relationship to economic evolution. Thus the German composer Hanns Eisler, best known for his works in collaboration with Bertolt Brecht, states that "all music is as much the reflection of political life as of social relations, even if this has not been the musician's intention at all. Music is the product of society, and in a manner of speaking the musician acts as the executive organ of society. A new type of artist would be one who would not be content merely to reflect social relations but would also endeavor to change them." But it is precisely because he tries to be this new type of artist who revolutionizes his technique, thereby hoping to further human progress, that Hanns Eisler, who, as an admirer and disciple of Arnold Schönberg, adopted the latter's twelve-tone system of composition, is accused by the Party of having embraced the error of formalism, a hydra whose heads grow back the moment Party doctrinarians cut them off.

Music has proved to be decidedly resistant to any sort of political interpretation. Soviet music critics make both a disturbing and a comforting spectacle of themselves when they gravely ponder whether such and such a theme in Shostakovich's Tenth Symphony celebrates the heroism of the Soviet people or whether on the contrary the dissonance of this theme condemns the barbarism of the imperialist enemy. Having tired of the quarrel and being anxious to have at its disposal musical works that Marxist esthetics could be certain would serve its purposes, the Central Committee of the Communist Party adopts Zhdanov's proposal in 1948 and decrees that the creations of all the great Soviet composers, Prokofiev, Shostakovich, Myaskovsky, and others, do not conform to the standards governing Soviet cultural life. Zhdanov himself demands that composers abandon any sort of formalism, give up writing symphonies that confuse people, and in the future write operas, oratorios, and songs whose text will be proof of their creators' Party loyalties. Shostakovich complies immediately; but ironically, his road to Damascus, instead of leading him to a Marxist conception of music, takes him back to a traditional conception, which from the point of view of Marxism is a bourgeois one.

Even cinema, despite its exceptional possibilities as an educational tool, which led Lenin to remark that it was "the most important of all the arts for the Revolution," poses thorny problems for Marxist esthetics: how can the purely visual aspect of the action depicted on the screen be prevented from overshadowing the lesson that this action is supposed to teach? The celebrated film-maker S. M. Eisenstein seems to have been quite willing to conform to the most rigid Marxist strictures. "Our conception of cinema is this: to reproduce life in all its truth, all its nakedness, and bring to light its social import and its philosophical meaning," he states. Nonetheless he too, or rather his exceptional talent, is considered highly suspect. Because of his use of new techniques such as montage and closeups, he is accused of formalism, and in 1948 he is summoned before a tribunal, along with Trauberg, Pudovkin, and other great film directors of the revolutionary era, and judgment is passed on them according to the sacrosanct canons of Socialist Realism. They are told that rather than concerning themselves with the visual quality of the image on the screen, they must devote all their attention to the quality of their dialogue.

As for Soviet painting, which is painfully mediocre (Russians admittedly have never excelled in this domain), a twofold pressure is brought to bear on it: both the choice of subject matter and the title of paintings must be "realistic." It must be indicated, for example, that children shown feeding pigeons are young champions of peace.

Marxist writers on esthetics are really comfortable only in the field of literature: in this domain it is easy to make hard and fast pronouncements and to establish a firm dictatorship over subject matter. Thus Marxist criticism is centered for the most part on literary problems. Girnus, an East German theoretician of Socialist Realism, attempts to justify this preference, which is dictated by purely tactical considerations, by stressing the philosophical reasons militating in favor of the primacy of literature. "We are thinking principally of belles-lettres," he writes. "It seems to me that it is important to emphasize the fact that they are the prime mover in the system of the arts. Why? Because language is the basis of their means of representation and because no other form of artistic expression is as intimately linked to language as literature (the basis of vocal compositions, of opera, of film is precisely linguistic material). Art is said to be the product of thinking in images. This is quite true. But this statement must be amplified by adding to it the following phrase of Karl Marx: 'Language is the immediate reality of thought.' I believe that the word 'immediate' in that phrase should be particularly stressed. In belles-lettres the representation of thought translated into an artistic image is immediately produced in the 'natural medium' of thought, that is to say language. The linguistic concept and the artistic image fuse in an indissoluble unity in the work of art. This is precisely what constitutes the particular power of literature as an artistic genre: for language is the most universal, the most precise, the most supple, and the most highly differentiated instrument of human—and therefore artistic—expression. Neither plaster nor marble nor metal nor color nor musical notes can compete with it in this respect. That is why literature, which uses this instrument to express artistic ideas, maintains its position as the highest of all the arts."

This demonstration nonetheless presupposes the premise that it purportedly proves. In order for literature to be recognized as the highest art, the theoretician must be persuaded a priori that art itself, far from being the "contemplation of things that do not depend on the principle of reason" which Schopenhauer speaks of, is simply the sensible appearance of the Idea. This is, in fact, Hegel's view of art. The conclusion that will necessarily follow from this vision of art is foreordained in his system. Just as in his system art is superseded first by religion and then by philosophy, so that it has rightfully been said that all of his *Esthetics* is merely a funeral sermon on art, so the hierarchy of the arts established by Marxist esthetics on the basis of their intelligibility can lead only to the subordination of art and the artist to the imperatives of a philosophical, or often a purely political, doctrine.

2

Dialectics

If we go straight to the various Marxist theoreticians and directly examine their statements and studies having to do with art and literature, if we survey all these opinions that only rarely concur, that in certain instances are complementary but in most cases are contradictory, we are forced to conclude that Marxist esthetics is almost impossible to understand. Rather than attempting to extrapolate this esthetics from the widely divergent interpretations of Marxist doctrine, would we not be better advised to take that doctrine itself as our point of departure, especially in view of the fact that it claims to be an all-embracing view of human reality whose multiple aspects can be understood only if they are consistently dealt with from the point of view of the whole?

If we adopt such an approach, we see that the essential subject matter of Marxist esthetics is the complex dialectics governing the interrelations of the work of art and human life. We know that from the Marxist point of view the basic structures of this life, which is regarded as the totality of human relations, depends upon economics, a term that embraces all man's efforts to master and exploit nature. There is a fundamental parallelism between this underlying economic structure and the various ideologies, be they political, religious, artistic, or philosophical; in principle, any given infrastructure will have a corresponding superstructure with the same characteristics. Hence the dominant ideas of each historical period must always be interpreted as the ideas of a class that a certain economic system has made the predominant power.

This totality, which Marxism takes as its special object of investigation, must not be regarded as a unity obtained by reducing it to the economic factor alone however. It is, rather, a potential totality, composed of elements that are quite diverse and sometimes contradictory, but nonetheless all tending toward ultimate convergence. The superstructures, in fact, do not depend exclusively on their common base; in addition to the common influence that the economic infrastructure has on them, they all interact on each other, and even affect the underlying economic structure that has produced them. Marxism thus puts us on our guard not only against any sort of idealistic conception that commits the error of separating the superstructures from their infrastructure, but also against any mechanistic temptation to disregard the dialectical relations between the base and the superstructures, on the one hand, and between the various superstructures on the other.

Friedrich Engels' letter of January 25, 1894, to Heinz Starkenburg makes this point in the clearest of terms: "Political, juridical, philosophical, religious, literary evolution, etc., is based on economic evolution. But they all react on each other, and also react on the economic base. The economic situation is not the *cause,* it is not the *sole agent* and all the rest merely a passive effect; rather there is a reciprocal effect stemming from economic necessity which *ultimately* is always the determining factor."

Once the fetishism of economics is exorcised, it is easy for Marxism to grant a relative autonomy to art and literature. For even though the artist or the writer is molded by his social experience and is influenced, either consciously or unconsciously, by the esthetic norms of the society to which he belongs, he is nonetheless first and foremost a creator, and through his activity contributes in turn to the effort to raise man above his animal state by arousing in men's minds and hearts the hope and the will to enhance the real, that is to say the realizable, potential of mankind, thus offering in his work a vision of the future possibilities inherent in the world.

It is this activity of the subject, this definition of the work of art as a reflection of the ongoing labor of successive generations, this continuing material creation aimed at the flowering of all human life that the young Marx clearly outlines in his 1884 manuscript, *Political Economy and Philosophy.* "It is only by the objective unfolding of the rich potential of the human being that the richness of human, subjective materiality, that a musical ear, an eye sensitive to the beauty of forms, that man's enjoyment, in a word, and man's receptive senses become *meanings* that manifest themselves as strengths of the human being, and are either developed or produced," he writes.

Once this perspective of the upward progress of mankind

is adopted, the aim of art becomes that of awakening humanity from its animal slumbers, of furthering the knowledge of itself that it acquires little by little, of revealing all man's potential resources. The truth of art then becomes synonymous with the self-awareness of the human species. "The education of the five senses is the work of all past generations," Marx writes in this same text. "A sensibility attuned to nothing but basic needs is thus only a limited sensibility. For men dying of starvation the human form of foods does not exist, but only their abstract forms as foods; they might just as well exist in the very crudest form, and it is hard to see any difference between this sort of feeding and that of animals. A man who is burdened with material cares, who is suffering great hardships cannot appreciate even the most beautiful spectacle; the seller of precious minerals is aware only of their market value, not their particular beauty; he has no mineralogical appreciation; thus the objectification of the human being, from both the theoretical and the practical point of view, is necessary in order to make man's senses *human,* and also to create the *human meaning* corresponding to all the rich potential of the human and natural being."

When art is regarded as a creative act that depends on human choice, thus re-establishing the prerogatives of the individual, we may well wonder how Marxist esthetics differs from preceding esthetics. Isn't Kant's *Critique of Judgment* also based on a philosophical analysis of the activity of the esthetic subject as a productive and receptive activity? But because his philosophical system is a form of subjective idealism, Kant is concerned only with the isolated individual. Marxist esthetics, on the other hand, endeavors to take into account the participation of creative individuals in the common effort of mankind to perfect a world that is seeking its own appropriate inner rhythm.

Like other esthetics before it, Marxist esthetics holds that art is neither a recollection of what has existed in the past nor a copy of what already exists, but a symbolic projection that bares the future and thus reveals the creative powers of mankind. But whereas preceding esthetics were cautiously limited to a groping empiricism, Marxist esthetics seeks to reveal the meaning and the effect of the efforts of artists and writers of every period of history. Espousing one of the beliefs of Hegelian philosophy, Marxism maintains that this growth in awareness is bound to lead to deeper understanding and clearer vision. Marxist esthetics not only makes it possible to preserve all the treasures of the past because it reveals the continuity of a genuinely realistic tradition that extends from antiquity to Socialist art and literature, but also so enlightens the artist or the writer that he will immediately find the highroad leading to conscious creative activity. "In the domain of esthetics, literary theory, and literary history," George Lukacs writes in his *Introduction to the Esthetic Writings of Marx and Engels,* "we can thus sum up the situation by saying that Marxism raises those principles of creative labor that have been alive for thousands of years in the system of the best thinkers and in the works of the most eminent writers and artists to the rank of enlightened concepts."

We must add, however, that even though the autonomy granted cultural activity serves to shield it against a crude sort of sociological analysis, the danger that it will be put in the exclusive service of the Party still remains. One might even maintain that it is precisely insofar as art and literature are freed from every other sort of subjection that they become more readily available for the propagation and the defense of a political policy. That is the conclusion that suggests itself, at any rate, when we read Stalin's article entitled "Marxism and Questions of Language." The author is quite willing to concede that for the most part literary activity is not subject to the involuntary servitude demanded of the remainder of the superstructure, but literature is granted this concession only in order that all the sovereign means at its disposal may be enrolled in support of political policies. Lukacs places particular emphasis on this political commitment of literature in his commentary on Stalin's text: "Every literary work, through the style of its language, its grouping of images and words, its rhythm, etc., must produce in us associations of ideas, feelings, and moods, evoke events and thoughts capable of mobilizing us for or against something."

In order to provide a firm foundation for the creative freedom of the esthetic subject, that freedom must not only be grounded in the general notion of praxis; it is also imperative to prove that esthetic activity does not necessarily develop according to the same pattern as other activities, that within human praxis there are many sequences, each of which obeys its own particular rhythm. This is the celebrated "law of uneven development" whose various applications Marx and Engels took particular pains to describe in detail.

In his letter of October 27, 1890, to Carl Schmidt, Engels

emphasizes the fact that a gap between philosophy and economic evolution has developed a number of times in history. He draws his correspondent's attention to the fact that often countries which were economically backward were in the very forefront in the area of philosophy. This was true of France, for instance, in the eighteenth century. Though England was far more advanced economically, France more than caught up with her in the realm of philosophy by taking as her point of departure the very philosophical system first developed in England, and later Germany occupied this same pre-eminent position in relation to France and England.

Marx regards the multiplicity of artistic forms and their quasi-autonomy as a possible explanation for the temporary gap that may exist between the evolution of these forms and the development of the infrastructure. Thus the epic, a genre which in the beginning is based on memory and oral transmission, necessarily belongs to an inferior level of art; it does not attain its classical form until written transmission gives it definite, fixed characteristics as a genre. "With regard to art," Marx writes in his introduction to *The Critique of Political Economy,* "we know that certain periods in which it flourished bear no relationship to the general evolution of society, and thus to the material base which is the skeleton, so to speak, of its organization. The Greeks as compared to the moderns, for example, or even to Shakespeare. As regards certain forms of art, the epic for instance, it is in fact a commonplace that they can never again be produced in their original form once their artistic production as such has entered the picture, and therefore within the realm of art in and of itself certain forms are possible only at a lower level of artistic development. Since this is true with regard to the relationship between the various artistic genres within the realm of art itself, it is even less surprising that this is also true with regard to the relationship of the entire realm of art as a whole to the general evolution of society."

The complexity of the overall relationship of art to the society of the period to which it belongs, of which Marx speaks at the end of the above-quoted passage, is illustrated by Engels by citing specific examples from a number of texts. Thus in a discussion of the novels that appear in the late classical period, Engels states that the theme of idyllic love so prominently featured in these works, far from reflecting the commonly accepted manners and morals of the society of the time, could have flourished only on the margin of that society, that their heroes were slaves who could not have shared the personal liberties or participated in the social activities of free citizens. The novel that later will reflect the violent conflicts of bourgeois society is in fact a product of the decline of the Greek and Roman social order.

In his correspondence with Paul Ernst, the young friend and disciple of Arnold Holtz, one of the founders of Naturalist drama, Engels taxes the latter with having endeavored to make Ibsen out to be a "petty-bourgeois" by analogy with members of that class in Germany, whereas Ibsen should rightfully be judged only on the basis of the specific evolution of society in Norway.

The question of the divergence between economic evolution and cultural evolution also involves the possibility that the artist may have a split personality, having one outlook as a member of society and an entirely different one as a creator. Hence both Marxist esthetics and Marxist doctrine as a whole are confronted with the problem of the "false consciousness," that is to say a consciousness which does not evaluate the pressures of society correctly and thus either attributes too much importance to the subjective factor, as in subjectivism, or else considers it to be totally ineffective, as in mechanistic conceptions. Because of its class situation, the proletariat, naturally, is uniquely privileged in that its consciousness of the realities of the situation is absolutely correct. "It [i. e., the proletariat] has no ideals to realize; all it need do is give free expression to the elements of the new society that have already been developed within the bourgeois society that is falling apart," Marx writes in *The Civil War in France*. This is not the case, however, for other classes, intellectuals in particular, who are convinced that the intellect is all-powerful and therefore regard consciousness and praxis, that is to say concrete human activity, as two separate and distinct things. In order to explain the origins of "false consciousness," Marx in his *German Ideology* goes back to the division of labor: "The division of labor becomes a real division only when a distinction between material and mental labor arises. From this moment on, consciousness can be effectively persuaded that something else exists besides the consciousness of existing praxis."

Literature, however, escapes the limitations of this false consciousness. Great works are never cast in the partisan mold of a single class; they express the relationships of various classes within society as a whole, enabling their authors to rise above their class biases, in a manner of speaking.

Thus a writer may very well prove to be a political conservative as an individual, and the author of a progressive work as an artist. As a man, he belongs entirely to his class, whose ideology he shares completely, whereas as an artist or a writer who has become aware of the dialectic of history, he brings to light the objective elements, the real dynamic forces underlying social evolution.

It is this truth inherent in literary praxis that Engels never ceases to admire in Balzac's novels. Since he was an ardent supporter of the old social order, why is it that Balzac offers us such a grim picture of the aristocracy of his time in his works? "The fact that Balzac was forced to act contrary to his own class sympathies and contrary to his own political biases," Engels writes in his famous 1888 letter to Miss Harkness, "the fact that he recognized the irreversible nature of the decline of his beloved aristocrats and depicted them as men who do not deserve a better fate, the fact that he glimpsed the real men of the future in the only place where it was possible to find them in my opinion constitute one of the greatest triumphs of realism and one of the most magnificent traits of old Balzac."

Marx goes even further. He admires Balzac not only because he revealed the social reality of his time but also because he depicted the future that inevitably awaits that society. "Balzac was not only the historian of the society of his time but also the prophetic creator of types which were merely in an embryonic state during the reign of Louis-Philippe and developed fully only after his death, in the reign of Napoleon III," Marx writes his son-in-law Paul Lafargue.

By maintaining that a consciousness that is "false" or

"biased" from the political or philosophical point of view can nonetheless go hand in hand with a consciousness that reflects reality quite accurately from the artistic point of view, Marx and Engels would seem to singularly diminish the propaedeutic value of a Marxist esthetic. Why should the writer bother to acquire a Marxist view of social reality when the proper exercise of his craft will lead him more or less automatically to see beyond his class situation and enable him to give the total living texture of his works not only the dimensions of contemporary reality but also to indicate the direction in which reality is heading, that is to say to envision the future?

In coming to grips with this problem that becomes a particularly acute one from the moment that Marxism becomes an official State doctrine, George Lukacs provides a twofold answer which is self-contradictory by the very fact that it is divided into two parts. On the one hand, he demands that the writer espouse a Socialist vision of the world, for "being a much more complete and much more profound vision than any other, it provides the writer a point of view that is clear-sighted enough to reflect and to represent social existence and social consciousness, men and human relations, the problems that confront human life and the solutions inherent in them." But on the other hand, he remains faithful to the teachings of Marx and Engels in that he concedes that a false consciousness, however idealistic it may be, in no way constitutes an obstacle to the creation of realistic works. Didn't Lenin himself one day tell Gorky that "an artist can extract from any philosophy many things that are useful to him, even though that philosophy may be idealistic"?

As for George Lukacs' intimate convictions regarding the political commitment of the writer, they do not appear to be very difficult to discern. His passionate interest in the great realists of the nineteenth century and in Thomas Mann is well known. His numerous reservations with regard to so-called Socialist literature are also well known. Though he airily maintains that a proper awareness, that is to say a loyalty to Party decisions, is a necessary condition for the creation of a literary work that enables us to glimpse the future, he hastily adds that this proper awareness is far from being a sufficient condition. In his opinion, literary creation is not dependent on such an awareness. "It would be a fatal error," he writes, "to believe that the process of transforming a true consciousness into a proper, realistic, and artistic reflection of reality is in principle more direct and simpler than that of transforming a false consciousness." Thus despite certain apparent concessions he has made under pressure from the Party, the truth for Lukacs, the defender of an open Marxist esthetics, remains a function of the literary work in and of itself, and criticism of literary activity in his eyes obeys internal criteria that are different from purely political criteria.

Within Marxist esthetics itself the relations between ideology and the creative work are the object of two definitions which in the beginning would seem to converge, but which ultimately come to represent two markedly divergent positions, especially after the discussions preceding the adoption of Socialist Realism as the official Party position in 1934.

The first of these is the definition of the position usually referred to as "the tendency" (*Tendenz*). Marx and Engels borrow this term from the Young Germany movement, which uses it to describe a literature with a progressive bias or "tendency" as opposed to pure art. But even though Marx and Engels adopt the word itself, they endeavor to give it a new meaning. In their eyes it is not a question of viewing the creative work from two different points of view, the ethical point of view represented by the term "tendency" and the esthetic point of view to be more or less arbitrarily described as having a certain political or social coloration, but rather of intimately connecting the work with its "social praxis," that is to say, demonstrating the profound, indissoluble unity between the writer's moral duty and the evolution of society.

The writer makes a mistake when he superimposes his own opinions on his work directly and immediately instead of baring the internal and dialectical laws of reality. The "tendency" is compatible with art and literature only if it is an organic product of the artistic essence of the work. That is what Engels specifically states in a letter to Kautsky dated November 26, 1885: "I am not absolutely opposed to tendency poetry as such. Aeschylus, the father of tragedy, and Aristophanes, the father of comedy, were both poets with a marked tendency, as were Dante and Cervantes, and the best thing about Schiller's *The Cabal and Love* is the fact that it is the first German drama with a political tendency. Today's Russians and Norwegians, who write excellent novels, are all tendency poets. But I am of the opinion that the tendency must be born of the situation and the action themselves without our attention being expressly drawn to it, and the poet is not obliged to provide the reader with the future historical solution of the historical conflicts that he depicts." In another letter addressed to a writer, Engels outlines even more clearly how necessary it is for the writer to allow the reality evoked in the work to reveal its own essence: "I am far from believing that you are at fault for not having written an authentic Socialist novel, a tendency-novel as we Germans call it, promoting the author's own political and social views. That is not at all what I meant. The more carefully concealed the author's opinions are, the better it is for the work of art," he writes.

Marx's criticism of Lassalle's tragedy is based in large part on the dissociation between action and ethics that he believes he has detected in this work. Far from appearing to be the inevitable consequence of the action unfolding on the stage, this ethic is expressed by way of set speeches that the author arbitrarily places in the mouths of those characters whom he has chosen as his spokesmen; according to Marx, Lassalle ought to have allowed the heroes of his tragedy the possibility of being faithful to their own selves, of testing their capabilities to the very limit, of exploring the internal, organic dialectic of their own personalities. "At the time you could have done much more to assure that the most modern ideas were given a hearing in their purest form, whereas looking back now, outside of *religious* freedom, bourgeois unity is the principal ideal expressed," he writes to Lassalle on April 19, 1895. "You should have automatically followed Shakespeare's example more closely, whereas your most serious fault in my opinion is the fact that you followed Schiller's example, that is to say you transformed individuals into mere exemplars of the spirit of the period."

The second position bears the name of "Party spirit" (*partignost*). This term, used by Lenin to describe the spirit that ought to govern the press and Party literature, later becomes the watchword of Socialist Realism. By contrast with the formalist deviation of the "tendency," which consists of draping alienated reality in bright Socialist banners and thus merely papering over the unbridgeable gap between "eternal duty" and a world that is inhuman by definition, the Party spirit enables the writer or the artist to bring the dynamics of a society that is naturally tending toward Socialism into the full light of consciousness. He thus actively collaborates in leading society to progress beyond the capitalist era whose internal contradictions prevent the spread of culture. Since the Party spirit is more or less inherent in social reality, it is possible to describe this reality as "the Party spirit of objectivity."

But this liberal conception of the Party spirit which follows the guidelines established by Marx and Engels fairly closely and adopts the same ideas concerning truth in literary praxis even though it cloaks them in a different form, is gradually supplanted by a narrow political conception as Marxist esthetics becomes more and more regimented after the 1930's. The Party spirit then loses its somewhat abstract character that leaves it open to the very broadest of interpretations simply because it is abstract. It becomes the exclusive point of view of the proletariat, the only class, according to Marxist doctrine, in a position to end all alienation because it is the class that has suffered the greatest degree of alienation itself, and thus the only class that by its very nature necessarily has a Socialist outlook. It is therefore the duty of the artist and the writer to side with those men whom Marx described in the *Communist Manifesto* as "bringing to light and ensuring in the various national struggles of the proletariat the triumph of the interests of the proletariat as a whole which are common and independent of nationality, on the one hand, and at the same time consistently representing the interests of the total movement in the different stages of evolution of the struggle between the proletariat and the bourgeoisie."

In accordance with tactics inspired by considerations which in most instances no longer have anything to do with purely cultural needs, Marxist esthetics thus wavers between encouraging a vision of the totality of human life which must be stripped of its alienating mask on the one hand, and a strict dependence on the proletariat, which is tantamount to blind submission to party directives, on the other. But the moment that it is recognized that a true Marxist esthetics must be based first and foremost on the continual application of dialectics, that what is required is not enrolling it in the service of a reality that in the beginning is reduced to the dimensions of the needs of one class but rather deciphering the inherent meaning of this class within a totality made up of its past, present, and future experiences, this esthetics leads to a Socialist humanism whose supreme rules are the passionate search for the very essence of humanity and the defense of human wholeness against all the dislocations and all the pitfalls of history. Such a conception of esthetics will place no restrictions on writers who may profess different political opinions but in the end share an objectivity which Lukacs describes in *The Historical Novel* as arising "organically" from the "struggle of historical forces within the objective reality of human society." Such a conception ultimately makes subjective value the only criterion, for only great writers possessed of an absolutely uncompromising conscience and willing to sacrifice everything for their art are capable of engaging in a literary effort of this magnitude and practicing an ideological objectivity that may be at odds with their own personal preferences.

"When the artistic development inherent in the situations and the characters imagined by the great realists runs counter to their own cherished biases, and even their most intimate convictions, they do not hesitate for an instant to abandon these biases and convictions and describe what they really see. This cruelty toward their own image of the immediate subjective world constitutes the most profound professional morality of the great realists, as opposed to those minor writers who almost always succeed in reconciling their own vision of the world with reality," Lukacs writes in *Balzac and French Realism*.

3

Form and Content

Marxist esthetics, which considers the work of art to be intimately related to social life as a whole, is left no choice with regard to the relation between content and form. It is forced to admit the priority of content, which then creates the need for an appropriate form. Marxist esthetics is therefore necessarily an esthetics centered on content; and thus is situated at the opposite pole from all esthetics based on a gratuitous or arbitrary play of forms and also from any sort of formalism. The relations between content and form correspond to the more general relations between the economic base and the ideological superstructure; content is the governing factor, and though form in the final analysis is always necessarily subservient to it, it is not thereby shorn of all autonomy whatsoever.

Hegelian esthetics reserves the highest praise for the unity of form and content, which becomes a revelation of the Idea, and the degree of unity achieved serves as a measuring rod of the perfection of a work of art. In his *Encyclopedia,* published in 1827, Hegel distinguishes three periods of art, the second of which represents the peak of artistic achievement. Viewing art in terms of the relationship between the Idea and its sensible appearance, he finds that in the first phase, which he calls the symbolist period, these two aspects of art have not yet fused: the content is still too abstract to engender its proper form. This is the period dominated by Oriental societies, previous to the birth of classical culture. It is during the second phase, which Hegel calls the classical period, that a living unity between form and content is achieved: interiority, having become more concrete, cries out for exteriorization, in a manner of speaking. In the third phase, which encompasses the Middle Ages and modern times, art founders in the seas of Romanticism. The infinite Idea can no longer be actualized except "in the infinite of intuition, whose characteristic mobility at each instant undermines and dissolves every concrete form." Inasmuch as Romanticism considers any concern for content as old-fashioned, art gradually becomes an entirely gratuitous exercise, an autonomous realm completely apart from life.

If we stand the Hegelian dialectic "on its head" and substitute social reality for the Hegelian Idea, this demonstration can serve equally well as an illustration of a fundamental concept of Marxist esthetics. Romanticism then becomes synonymous with the capitalist era whose internal contradictions cause the nature of reality to be completely accidental; since any comprehension of the overall mechanisms of human life therefore becomes impossible, artistic form no longer has any reference to any specific content. By stressing the dialectical relationship of form and content within a reality that is again comprehensible, Marxist esthetics safeguards art against a twofold danger: that of a naturalism in which content is shorn of form, and that of a formalism which gives up all concern for content in order to engage in all manner of experiments with pure form, which then develops completely independently.

The equation established by Hegelian esthetics between the Beautiful and the True is attacked, however, by "social" or "civic" criticism (*obshchestvenny*), particularly as practiced by the Russian radical critics Belinsky, Chernyshevsky, and Dobrolyubov, who lived in the nineteenth century but whose influence becomes greater and greater as Marxism triumphs in their native land. Though they are quite willing to grant that there are certain relationships between the social reality and the art of any given period (these critics call to mind Plekhanov's admiration of Hegel's interpretation of seventeenth-century Dutch painting), they nonetheless reject the Hegelian conception of Beauty as the sensible appearance of the Idea. Culture and esthetics, art and life appear to them to be irreconcilable opposites. Art in their eyes is merely a form of enjoyment restricted to the nobility and therefore an insult to the suffering lower classes. Through the strong influence of this typically Russian critical attitude, wherein the attack on the bad conscience of the aristocracy is reinforced by Rousseauism, Marxist esthetics begins to tend more and more toward a total indifference to outward form, and the entire emphasis is placed on the need for a specifically social content.

V. G. Belinsky (1810–1848), who is described by Turgenev as "the Russian Lessing," has exercised a twofold influence on Marxist esthetics. In his 1834 *Literary Reveries,* allowing himself to be guided by Schelling's metaphysics and esthetics, he notes that writers are men "capable of fully expressing the spirit of the people among whom they were born and raised." We know how important contemporary Marxist esthetics considers popular art, and popular dances in particular. "The spirit of the people," a concept Belinsky borrows from Schelling and enthusiastically champions, thus partially overshadows the "party spirit of objectivity" that the proletariat represents.

Belinsky's 1846 work entitled *Views on Literature* advances a number of points in a closely argued refutation of Hegelian esthetics. Belinsky's main premise is that "art is the recreation of reality; therefore its role is not to correct or embellish life, but to show it as it really is." This is proof of his rejection of the Hegelian thesis that the Beautiful and the True are essentially synonymous.

The high point of Belinsky's criticism, which deals with a great number of writers whose activity he judges not from an absolute point of view but on the basis of the social circumstances that have influenced them and consequently shaped their work, is the contrast he establishes between Pushkin (1799–1837), who represents the end of an era, and Gogol (1809–1852), who opens the new era of critical realism. Whereas Pushkin, whose one concern is the beautiful, which he is led by the notion of art for art's sake to celebrate as the supreme value, reflects the ideology of the nobility, Gogol, who is concerned about social questions, regards beauty and ethics as two separate and distinct things in his *Nevsky Prospekt*.

This separation of the good and the beautiful is all the more justified in Belinsky's view in that the beautiful is incapable of influencing real life and correcting its injustices. Thus Belinsky is of the opinion that esthetics must have a moral basis that lies outside of the realm of art; in the end he calls upon religion to point out the moral obligations of art. Pure art in his view is merely an attempt to escape and to forget, a sort of desertion in the face of the demands of social life, and must give way to artistic creation that endeavors to collaborate in "the common task," that is to say the transformation of life in such a way as to ensure the triumph of the religious ideal.

Belinsky's ambivalent attitude toward Hegelian esthetics could not help but enhance the influence that he was later to exercise on the Marxist esthetics being developed by Russian theorists. The economic evolutionism which he introduces into literary history causes Plekhanov to remark that Belinsky remained faithful to Hegel despite his spectacular break with him, at least insofar as his dialectic was concerned. However, when social utilitarianism, which does away with the dialectical nature of this economic evolutionism and thus imposes arbitrary limits on it, is introduced into a Marxist esthetics, it causes this esthetics to take entirely the wrong turn, to the point that it becomes merely a propaganda tool.

Like Belinsky, N. G. Chernyshevsky (1828–1889) stresses the national nature of literary activity. Since the purpose of art is to reflect reality, Russian art and literature must be an absolutely faithful mirror of Russian life, with no fancy frills whatsoever. That is why he forbids Russian writers to use literary devices borrowed from German Romanticism or from any other foreign literature. Moreover, by maintaining that "the beautiful is life," or in any event "life as it should be," he too eventually embraces a sort of economicism wherein the work of art should not be an expression of the subjectivity of the artist but an instrument of economic and social evolution. Art in his view is justified only insofar as it is useful; it must further genuine social progress.

But probably the most characteristic feature of Chernyshevsky's esthetics is his view that art is inferior to reality. Art is nothing but a more or less faithful imitation of reality; the very best works of art approach perfection but never actually attain it. His scorn for artistic form would appear at first sight to enhance the value of content by contrast; but in the final analysis his view of content is equally scornful, for once separated from form it is merely a pale reflection of a reality that continually eludes its grasp. Art thus is no different from science, which also endlessly stalks reality in its efforts to attain a clearer and clearer understanding of its complexities. "The defense of the superiority of reality by contrast with imagination," Chernyshevsky concludes in his work *The Esthetic Relationships of Art and Reality* (1855), "the effort to demonstrate that works of art are definitely incapable of withstanding comparison with living reality—that is the essence of our argument; but doesn't speaking of art as the author does here not imply the disparagement of art? Yes, if demonstrating that art is inferior to the reality of life as far as the artistic perfection of its works is concerned is tantamount to belittling art: but objecting to the panegyrics in its favor is not at all the same thing as disparaging it. Science does not regard itself as superior to reality and is not ashamed of its inferior status. Let art cease to consider itself superior to reality: such a status is not at all humiliating. Science is not ashamed to say that its aim is to understand and explain reality, and then apply these explanations for the good of mankind: art too should feel no shame at recognizing that its aim is to compensate man, should reality have failed to afford him complete esthetic enjoyment, by doing its utmost to reproduce this precious reality and to explain it for the good of mankind."

N. A. Dobrolyubov (1836–1865), the creator of so-called "à propos" criticism, that is to say criticism for which the literary work is only a pretext for dealing with the most diverse sorts of problems, also discusses the national or popular elements (*navodnost*) that have played a role in the evolution of Russian literature. He has a particularly high regard for Goncharov, whose novel *Oblomov* furthers the reader's understanding of certain typical features of the evolution of society in Russia. Oblomov's nihilism, his total rejection of the world, is an exceptionally cruel reflection of the fate of the individual who is lost in the morass of petty-bourgeois life in the provinces.

Dobrolyubov attaches much greater importance to the personal value of the artist than do Belinsky and Chernyshevsky. Though he grants that the primary mission of the artist is to reproduce reality and bare the problems inherent within it, Dobrolyubov is convinced that the fulfillment of this mission depends above all else on the subjectivity of the artist. It is out of his genius that the work will flower, for reality provides merely the concrete background of the work of art. "The artist," Dobrolyubov writes, "is not a photographic plate, reflecting only the present moment: if he were, the work of art would have neither life nor meaning. When the true artist goes about the creation of his work, he already possesses it, complete and entire, in his soul, with its beginning and its end, with its precious underlying motivations and its secret consequences, which logical thought cannot grasp but which the inspired gaze of the artist reveals."

The discussion of the work of art as a reflection that takes place within the realm of Russian criticism assumes even broader proportions when it is viewed from the perspective of Marxist esthetics as a whole. Marx and Engels are principally concerned with shedding light on the extremely complex dialectical relationships between the artistic subject and the object. Belinsky and Chernyshevsky, on the other hand, though still concerned with these relationships, essentially reduce them to an economic evolutionism, and thus place more emphasis on the object, which thereby acquires, if not a total autonomy, at least a clear superiority by comparison with the subject. We also see evidences of this same subtle shift of emphasis, which is obviously not a sharp break but nonetheless is something more than a mere extension of the previous line of argument, when we compare Marxism properly speaking with philosophical Leninism. In his study entitled *Materialism and Empiriocriticism,* Lenin rightly remarks that Marx and Engels "placed more emphasis on *dialectics* than on *materialism,* and when dealing with historical materialism, stressed the *historical* aspect more than the materialist aspect." But as an avowed opponent of the empiriocriticism of Mach and Avenarius which reduces the study of the material world to a descriptive inventory of sensations, an approach which had become a dangerous deviation once A. A. Bogdanov had made it a part of Marxist doctrine in his *Essay on the Philosophy of Marxism,* Lenin constantly emphasizes the priority of matter over consciousness, and insists that "objective reality exists independently of the human consciousness that reflects it."

In the final analysis the direction an esthetic takes depends on the theory of knowledge on which it is based. The objects of esthetics can be correctly interpreted only from the standpoint of the general conception of the object laid down by epistemological theory. From the moment that the critic begins to speak in terms of consciousness-as-a-reflection, that is to say of a consciousness whose only role is to copy and to photograph an objective reality that is outside of it and independent of it, the artistic subject no longer has any creative role to play and the problems inherent in the artistic object are no longer of any importance.

Faced with the problem of consciousness-as-a-reflection, a tenet it would like to incorporate for tactical reasons, Marxist esthetics turns back to the far less restrictive concepts of Marx and Engels. Engels in particular insists in his letter of April 1888 to Miss Harkness that realism is "over and above the fidelity of the details, the faithful reproduction of typical characters in typical circumstances." At first glance at least, Engels' statement would seem to imply that the artistic and literary mirroring of reality should not be confined to its objective surface appearances, but that the writer or artist should rather regard it as his principal task to seek out its true nature below that surface. If we take Engels' notion of the "typical" as our starting point, we find it fairly easy to follow the path leading to one of the fundamental categories of dialectical materialism, namely the relationships linking phenomena and their essence.

According to Marxist doctrine, essence is the sum total of the principal internal aspects of a process, whereas phenomena are the immediate outward expression of this process. The essence and phenomena are thus both related to the same process, and in this respect they are interdependent and indissociable. Lenin compares the essence to a deep current and phenomena to waves and swirls of foam that disturb its surface. "The foam [is] on top and the deep currents below. But the foam is also the expression of the essence," he states in his *Philosophical Notebooks*.

The prime task of Marxist esthetics, therefore, is to reestablish the dialectical unity of the essence and phenomena, in contradistinction to the tendencies of bourgeois esthetics, which disregards human totality and makes of the essence and phenomena two different levels of consciousness. According to George Lukacs, art must "provide an image of reality in which the counterpointing of phenomenon and essence, the exception and the rule, immediacy and the concept, etc., is so intimate a blend of the two opposites that they totally intermingle and form a spontaneous unity in the immediate impression we have of a work of art, constituting for the person experiencing them an indivisible unity."

By establishing interconnections between the essence and phenomena, art brings to light what is. We acquire a deeper knowledge of reality through this relationship that art establishes between hidden reality and surface reality. The mission of shedding such light is never-ending, however. The discovery of reality goes hand in hand with historical evolution, for the field of investigation broadens as the tools of research available to us become more and more numerous. The search for the "typical" becomes synonymous with the progressive rediscovery of life itself. "A type," Lukacs writes in *Balzac and French Realism,* "does not become a type because it represents the average, nor does it become such through its individual nature alone, however pronounced that nature may be, but rather because all the moments of a historical phase which are essential and determining factors from the human and social point of view converge and multiply within it so that the creation of the type reveals these moments at their highest point of development, at the outer limit of the unfolding of the possibilities concealed within them, in the starkest representation of extremes, giving concrete form both to the highest point of achievement and to the limits of mankind as a whole in a given period."

Insofar as Marxist esthetics seeks to restore the fundamental unity between the essence and phenomena, does it not risk regressing to the level of classical esthetics and returning to the hypothesis that there is such a thing as absolute Beauty? We know that Aristotle regarded beauty as the product of the structural ordering of a world that art progressively reveals; his esthetic is based on an ordering of the whole that is complete and organic, "resembling a living being." When we read certain of George Lukacs' pronouncements with regard to esthetics, we realize that this convergence between classical esthetics and Marxist esthetics is so complete at times that the two become totally fused and perhaps even totally confused. "The essential determinations of this world represented by a literary work of art," Lukacs writes at one point for instance, "are revealed . . . through an artistic succession and an artistic gradation. But this gradation must be achieved within the inseparable unity of the phenomenon and the essence, a unity that exists immediately, from the very outset; it must make this unity more and more intimate and obvious by making it more and more concrete."

If Marxist esthetics limited itself to pointing out the a priori existence of a unity between the essence and phenomena and if its sole mission were to remove the screen that conceals such a unity from us, it would continually run the risk of falling back into the sort of passive contemplation that is the hallmark of classical esthetics. In that case it would not differ in any essential way from Kantian esthetics, in which "taste is the faculty of judging an object or a mode of representation on the basis of satisfaction or dissatisfaction in a completely disinterested way," or from the "pure gaze of art on the world" which in Schopenhauer's philosophy momentarily delivers man from the will to live, the source of all his pain.

But it is precisely because Marxist esthetics never loses sight of the real richness of the world, that is to say its totality, the mastery of which will be the end-result of an evolutionary process that mankind has been involved in from the beginning of its history, precisely because it is conscious of the totality of human life, that this esthetics feels called upon to stress the unfinished nature of the world we live in, offering us, we might say, the image of the possibilities inherent in the existing state of affairs. Marxist esthetics must foster hope for a world that is at peace with itself, and therefore it must foster our firm determination to contribute to the realization of such a world. Like the philosophers discussed in the eleventh of Marx's *Theses on Feuerbach,* artists and writers "have merely *interpreted* the world in different ways when what is needed is to *transform* it."

In order for art to be able to carry out this investigation that Marxist esthetics assigns it, it is necessary to give it a privileged status. Art must not only somehow find a way around the obstacle put in its path by the notion of consciousness-as-a-reflection which makes it totally dependent on the object; that obstacle itself must be removed.

The very first step in that direction would be to determine exactly what Lenin meant by his statement that matter exists independently of consciousness. In point of fact, his real purpose was not so much to reduce the role of consciousness as to re-establish the importance of matter in the face of the empiriocriticism of Mach and Avenarius, which made matter quite secondary as compared to sensations. However thoroughgoing this materialism might appear to be, it successfully avoids the mechanist temptation and remains dialectical, that is to say it leaves a place for the reciprocal action of the elements that determine reality. Far from being reduced to a slavish dependence on matter, consciousness in fact is given back its rightful place at the very heart of the dialectical process.

Insofar as consciousness is granted a certain autonomy, the mission assigned it as a reflection of the world, the grasp of the world that it is capable of attaining, can take place in a number of different ways. George Lukacs, for instance, makes a fundamental distinction between the scientific reflection and the artistic reflection of reality. Whereas the former in his view provides a conceptual image of reality, the latter represents reality through the workings of imagination. Art therefore is not the product of a simple sort of perception, but of a perception reproduced by imagination, that is to say a re-presentation. If science places man face to face with reality itself, art offers "the mimetic reflection of reality." "Every esthetic reproduction of reality is full of emotions," Lukacs writes in *Particularity as an Esthetic Category* (1957), "not in the same way as in everyday life in which there are objects independent of consciousness the perception of which is accompanied by emotions, but rather in such a way that emotionality becomes an indispensable constitutive element in the artistic presentation of the object viewed in all its individual particularity. Every love poem is written for (or against) a woman (or a man), every landscape has a certain particular character which assures its fundamental unity and which expresses—in what is admittedly a very complex way—a positive or negative attitude with regard to reality and certain tendencies at work within it."

The distinction between scientific reflection and artistic

reflection reintroduces into Lenin's concept of consciousness-as-a-reflection the creative subjectivity that would appear to have been banished from it altogether. But are we here dealing with an interpretation which, though it is surprising in more than one respect, is nonetheless compatible with the general orientation of Marxist doctrine, or are we here face to face with a simple subterfuge, in the form of the apparent acceptance of a principle opposed to any sort of true esthetics, the aim of which is to safeguard at all costs the continued existence of subjectivity within a culture?

No matter how we approach the problem, we run a very great risk of encountering contradictions that are truly insurmountable. Since for Marxism artistic and literary praxis is an integral part of human praxis, it is difficult to see why art should be accorded a privileged position by granting it a particular nature that distinguishes it from other human activities. As for science, far from being reduced to a mere conceptualization of the world, it should be seen as playing much the same role in human praxis as art: doesn't science too continually seek out new techniques that it hands over to men eager to make nature submit to their bidding? But above all dealing with artistic reflection not in terms of the object, which necessarily possesses a historical content, but rather in terms of a timeless order of the imagination, threatens to focus esthetics on a sort of abstraction that is far removed from any kind of reality and thus quite incompatible with Marxist doctrine.

4

Revolutionary Art

The interdependence of form and content recognized by Marxist esthetics makes political and social revolution the driving force behind artistic conceptions. Thus for Franz Mehring, the best-known German Marxist critic, the development of a proletarian culture is impossible within bourgeois society; only a revolutionary transformation of reality can produce such a culture.

By creating a new political and social content, the October Revolution offers artists and writers an opportunity to seek new forms appropriate to an entirely new situation. The political and artistic avant-garde share the feeling that a new order is dawning, and both march toward the future with the same quickened pace. The more and more rapid flurry of political activities is accompanied by a constant improvement of artistic techniques. Russian tradition and Marxist doctrine, in fact, join hands to maintain and further the primacy of content. But this revolutionary content requires a revolutionary mold. According to the Marxist view, this new content should have given rise to a new form. As a matter of fact, the groundwork for this new form had been laid for some time, for the defeat of 1905 had plunged Russia into a prerevolutionary mood. Since the political hopes of intellectuals were disappointed, their determination to win emancipation now found expression in the realm of art, so that we would not be exaggerating the situation if we were to claim that artistic revolution in Russia preceded political revolution. It is precisely the birth of revolutionary artistic forms at a moment when the content is still bourgeois that later enables the Soviet regime, which after its consolidation is eager to adapt itself to the petty-bourgeois tastes of its bureaucracy, to transform the revolutionary upsurge of artistic forms during the first years of the regime into a rigid and simplistic neo-academicism, or worse still, to denounce the revolutionary confusion in the field of art as a manifestation of bourgeois decadence.

The variety of literary schools that appears in the wake of the Revolution is really most impressive; it ranges from enthusiasts who believe that they are witnessing the birth of a totally new world and therefore are anxious to start all over from zero, to indifferent theoreticians who regard esthetics as a refuge against continual demands that art be enrolled in the service of political action.

The "Proletkult" literary movement led by A. A. Bogdanov wishes to eliminate the past altogether. "In the name of our future we are burning Raphael, destroying the museums, and trampling on the flowers of art," is the fiery proclamation that accompanies the opening of centers for proletarian culture; writers and poets of the older generation who have rallied round the Revolution after having abjured the esthetic errors of the past take on the task of educating young working-class writers in these centers in order to create a purely proletarian literature. Around 1930 the "Proletkult" leads to the promulgation of the "Rapp doctrine" by the Russian Association of Proletarian Writers, aimed at creating an entirely new culture to fit the needs of the proletariat.

Lenin is not very much in favor of this group of writers who regard themselves as the avant-garde of Soviet literature whose mission it is to safeguard that literature from any sort of deviation. Far from approving of their iconoclasm, he stresses the importance of the cultural heritage in the creation of a proletarian culture. "If we do not clearly understand that a proletarian culture can be built only on the basis of a precise knowledge of the culture created by the entire evolution of humanity and by the integration of this culture, if we do not understand that, we cannot fulfill our task. Proletarian culture is not something that suddenly surfaces without our having any idea of where it comes from, it is not the invention of people who claim to be specialists in proletarian culture. All of that is preposterous. . . . All the culture that capitalism has left us must be carefully preserved and it is on this basis that Socialism must be built, otherwise it will be impossible for us to create the life of Communist society. And this science, this technique, and this art are in the hands and minds of specialists."

Like the members of the "Proletkult" movement, the Futurists have a negative attitude toward the past; they too are eager for a total break with bourgeois art. Their school profits enormously from the contributions of Mayakovsky (1895–1930), a genius who is able to impart an exceptional revolutionary fervor to an art expressly intended to appeal to the popular masses. During the years immediately following the October Revolution, literature seemed to have fallen on dark days for two reasons: political activity had become the first concern in every area of life, and the printing presses had almost shut down altogether because of a severe paper shortage. Mayakovsky, at once a revolutionary and a lyric poet, does not hesitate to walk the streets in order to acquaint the public with his "products." He does his utmost to aid the Revolution, reciting propaganda poems, writing and singing satirical songs anywhere and everywhere, in the streets, in cafes, at literary gatherings; he designs posters and organizes theatrical performances. This essentially oral period of Soviet literature, extending from around 1917 to 1920, thus sees the birth of a new lyricism amid the general hardships of the time. Though this new lyricism is not centered on strictly personal problems, it is fascinating nonetheless. Mayakovsky manages, in fact, to raise what would seem to be the most prosaic subjects in the world to the level of the purest poetry: in his hands the vocabulary of popular journalism, the language of the streets and the new simplified syntax take on an extraordinary luster. Mayakovsky tried hard to "put his foot on the throat of song," as he phrased it, referring to his hard-fought struggle against his own elegiac tendencies, but, far from destroying the lyricism of his work, this self-discipline enhanced it.

The political and social mission assigned to artists and writers by the leaders of the Revolution is carried out with particular zeal in the theater, under the brilliant leadership of Meyerhold, the director of the theatrical section of the People's Commissariat for Popular Culture. Lunacharsky, the first Soviet commissar of education, rightly claims that in Meyerhold's theatrical activity the esthetics and the politics of the left become so closely conjoined that they are inseparable.

Meyerhold had been engaged in all sorts of theatrical experiments long before the October Revolution. But it is only after the Revolution delivers him from every manner of theatrical convention and social constraint that his talents as a director are allowed absoutely free expression. In order to win the popular masses, who for the most part are illiterate, over to the cause of the Revolution, Meyerhold forms "theatrical shock troops" and has them perform very simple plays specially written for agitation and propaganda purposes. It is theater with a message, the aim of which is strictly didactic, a theater guided and directed by political considerations. But in order to keep these performances from being the boring and tiresome exercises that politically "committed" art all too often becomes, Meyerhold takes great pains to give them a form so new and so unusual that it will capture and hold the attention of the audience.

His staging, aimed at dramatizing and reinforcing the political lesson taught by the play, borrows many devices from periods in which theater was a popular genre, but at the same time it is based on a small number of fundamental principles that will later be followed more or less closely by the theater of the extreme left.

The acting is based on a principle that Meyerhold calls "bio-mechanics." As the word suggests, the actor must follow a certain fixed system of gestures to represent human emotion. Each gesture he uses is calculated with mathematical exactitude and has an immediate symbolic value. Thus sadness is represented by the actor's assuming just one attitude, which never varies: he bows his head, moves about very jerkily, and becomes careless about his dress. Joy, on the other hand, is expressed by breaking into a little dance step.

The aim of "bio-mechanics" is the total depersonalization of the various characters. Since the style of acting is not aimed at suggesting the individual character traits of the person the actor is playing, but rather the feeling or the emotion that this person shares with all the rest of humanity, the sort of socialization that is the goal of political action in real life is actually achieved to some degree on the stage. Meyerhold eventually has all his actors and actresses wear identical blue overalls, thus not only blurring individual differences in appearance but also making both sexes look alike. The only distinction that is maintained is that of class: the actors are taught a special technique of pantomiming and gesturing that enables them to show exactly what class the character they are playing belongs to.

The clown is a favorite character in Meyerhold's theater, thus marking a return to a popular Russian tradition. Whereas the theater of the West attracts audiences from the classes in power who find their own ideology mirrored in it, Meyerhold goes back to the circus tradition which is bound to have an immediate appeal to the proletariat. Moreover, the court jester, who by tradition is allowed to tell the Czar the most unpalatable truths, is regarded as a sort of revolutionary ancestor. To further enhance the popular appeal of his theater, Meyerhold uses all the acrobatic tricks and juggling acts traditionally associated with the figure of the clown. The clown role provides a convenient and enjoyable way of putting the serious political message across through parody and exaggeration, accusations so extreme as to be ridiculous, and slapstick disputations.

The staging itself is based on the principle of "dynamic constructivism." The traditional—and extremely artificial—conventions of the stage are done away with entirely. There is no curtain separating the actors from the audience, no prompter's box, no wings, no props. The spectators face a large space that from the beginning of the performance to the end has nothing in it but "constructions," that is to say scaffoldings, flights of steps, cubes, arches and so on, so that the action takes place within immense geometrical perspectives. This décor is not at all static however, for these "constructions" are continually shifted about, both horizontally and vertically, with the aid of moving platforms, escalators, electric tows, cranes, and all sorts of special mechanical devices invented by Meyerhold. As for the actors, they too participate in this "dynamic constructivism" by continually moving all over the stage area, not only back and forth but also up and down, scaling the scaffoldings and climbing up and down suspended ropes. Moreover, the stage area is constantly swept by spotlights, projected film sequences suddenly interrupt the actors, and at irregular intervals musicians strike up an accompaniment that includes everything from accordion tunes to jazz numbers.

Meyerhold's revolutionary staging is inspired in large part

by theatrical experiments that had been conducted long before the October Revolution and entirely apart from Marxist canons, for they were innovations of an avant-garde rebelling against bourgeois ideology. The Party therefore later came to regard Meyerhold's revolutionary drama as the last gasp of bourgeois decadence in the theater. It is possible nonetheless to reconcile Meyerhold's theatrical practices with a Marxist esthetics. If it is true that art reflects reality, Meyerhold was justified in ridding the stage of its clutter of illusionistic devices and making it over in the image of the setting in which the heroes of the Revolution, the proletariat, live their lives, namely factories and workshops filled with machines. Dynamic constructivism is the theatrical counterpart of the building of Socialism in the Soviet Union. "Our artists must abandon the brush," Meyerhold said, "and take up the compass, the axe, and the hammer, in order to rebuild the stage in the image of our technical world."

Moreover, if it is true that artistic praxis is one of the vital components of human praxis as a whole, the spectator should by all rights take an active part in the performance. "Dynamic" staging allows them to do exactly that. The spectators' imagination is kept continually on the alert because the action is constantly shifting from one place to another. Since there is nothing separating the spectators from the action being staged, it is possible for the actors to address them directly at all times, and therefore the performance that takes place is the common creation of the actors and the audience. "The aim of theater," Meyerhold insists, "is not to put a finished artistic product before an audience, but to make the spectator cooperate in the creation of the work.

The current must not only flow from the stage to the audience, but in the reverse direction as well."

One of the strangest phenomena in the history of literature in Russia following the October Revolution is the triumph of the Formalist school in the years 1921 to 1925. This movement in literary criticism spreads rapidly within the "Section for the History of Literature" founded in 1920 as a part of the State Institute for the History of Art in Saint Petersburg. Despite its semiofficial status, it deliberately adopts a critical position that is totally contrary to Marxist esthetics. The Formalist school, whose principal tenets are outlined in the collective work entitled *The Problems of Poetics,* which serves as a sort of manifesto of the movement, not only rejects any sort of biographical and psychological interpretation of a literary work, but is also particularly opposed to any kind of sociological interpretation; the only thing of interest to the Formalist critic is the poetic work itself, its composition, its rhythm, its metrics, and its style. The "Association for the Study of Poetic Language," which goes by the abbreviated name of "Opoyaz" and is headed by Shklovsky, thus totally disregards the content of a work and devotes itself exclusively to the study of specific literary techniques; the Word and the author's verbal strategies are regarded as much more important than the subject matter.

This most surprising new direction taken by Russian literary criticism, which had traditionally concerned itself only with content, would seem at first glance to be inspired by a firm determination to free literary criticism of its dependence on the sort of religious ideas that appear in Dostoevsky's work or in Berdyaev's philosophy. Because the Russians are the God-seeking people par excellence, even when they are overcome with the vertigo of a revolution whose spirit is supposedly entirely atheistic, they find it extremely difficult to rid themselves of the idea of divinity. Alexander Blok, the leader of the Russian Symbolist school, does not hesitate, for instance, to place Christ at the head of the Red Guards in his poem *The Twelve*. There were thus certain justifiable reasons why the Party regarded the "Opoyaz" as an ancillary critical school, for even though it did not obey Marxist principles, it nonetheless furthered them by attempting to totally eradicate other critical tendencies that ran counter to it. "The principal slogan around which the Formalists rallied," according to Boris Eichenbaum, one of the theoreticians of Formalism, "was that of the emancipation of poetic style and the refusal to bow to the philosophical and religious tendencies which were increasingly enslaving the submissive Symbolists."

But shortly thereafter the fundamentally anti-Marxist bias of Formalism is freely admitted and even proudly proclaimed by its followers. Boris Eichenbaum openly challenges the Party by categorically refusing to regard literature as a mere superstructure. In his view, any attempt to explain a work of literature in terms of any sort of economic or social science is tantamount to denying the autonomy or the internal dynamics of literature, to failing to take its evolution into account and paying attention only to its origins. Shklovsky for his part even goes so far as to dare to question the intimate connection between form and content that is a sacrosanct principle of Marxist criticism. "The forms of art are to be judged on the basis of their artistic legitimacy. A new form does not appear in order to express some new content, but to replace an older form that has lost its literary value," he writes in his *Theory of Prose*. And when Party doctrinaires who are up in arms against such heresy back him into a corner, he haughtily declares: "We are not Marxists, but if some day we were to have a need for such an implement, we would not eat with our hands out of sheer pride." Marxism for Shklovsky is what God was for the astronomer Laplace: "a hypothesis that thus far [he] had had no need of."

In the beginning at least, the Bolshevik leaders' attitude toward Formalism is rather ambivalent. In general these leaders are highly cultured men who are not inclined to be excessively dogmatic despite their unshakable loyalties to the revolutionary cause. They prefer to maintain a certain reserve; the most extreme step their Marxist convictions lead them to take is to utter rather timid condemnations in which the mitigating circumstances play a more important role than the supposed crime itself. Thus Bukharin willingly admits that the "Opoyaz" has fulfilled a certain propaedeutic role as a school of literary criticism insofar as it has attempted to draw up a "catalogue" of poetic devices. "This analytic activity must be given its due as a step toward a later critical synthesis," he writes with regard to the Formalist school. He refuses to concede, however, that Formalism is capable of achieving such a synthesis on its own.

Trotsky more or less embraces the views of the Formalist school when he concedes that Marxism, in and of itself, is incapable of providing the criteria of esthetic judgment. On the other hand, however, Marxism is the only philosophy that has offered a causal explanation of literature. "Only Marxism can explain why and how a certain orientation has arisen in art in any given historical period," he states. Hence the attempt of the Formalists to shed light on the particular artistic features of literary form is justifiable, but they are wrong when they attempt to reduce the whole of literature to its style of verbal expression; the task of the literary critic is not limited to an essentially descriptive, quasi-statistical analysis of the etymology and the syntax of a poem, and certainly not to a simple inventorying of its vowels and consonants. "The Formalists are disciples of Saint John. They believe that 'in the beginning was the Word.' But we believe: 'in the beginning was the Act. The Word came after, as its phonetic shadow,'" Trotsky writes.

Lunacharsky is the critic who would appear to have voiced the most severe criticism of the Formalist preoccupation with poetic devices rather than with content. Lunacharsky regards the literary criticism of Formalism as a type of "escapism," that is to say a way of avoiding real human problems and a sterile product of the decadent ruling class. "The only artistic genre that the modern bourgeoisie can enjoy and understand is nonobjective, purely formal art," he writes in *Formalism in Esthetics*. "In order to satisfy this need, narrow-minded bourgeois intelligence has produced both a brigade of Formalist artists and an auxiliary corps of estheticians whose orientation is Formalist." And in his discussion of the Russian Formalist school in particular, he adds this remark which foreshadows the thunderbolts that the Party will eventually launch against a movement whose very name will one day become a senseless dirty epithet, the evil epitome of everything that is opposed to the beneficent influence of Socialist Realism: "Before October, Formalism was a vegetable that was in season. Today it is a stubborn vestige of the *status quo,* an ultimate refuge of intelligence which has not yet been transformed and which slyly winks out of the corner of its eye at the European bourgeoisie."

In the period immediately following the year 1917, Marxist esthetics, borne on the wings of revolutionary enthusiasm, thus forges ahead in a number of very different directions. Although in principle the "Proletkult" enjoys a sort of state monopoly of culture, the independence and freedom of artistic and literary creation are fervently defended by Gorky, Lunacharsky, and Trotsky. The 1925 resolution of the Central Committee still recognizes the right of those whom Trotsky calls "the literary fellow travelers on the road to Russian Revolution" to study man's inner world independently of political and historical considerations. In the era of speeded-up rhythms of production, the novelist Yury Olesha has one of his heroines defend the view that "the artist must think slowly," thus openly opposing the Marxist dogma that insists that economic and literary evolution must proceed hand in hand. The baroque, epic writer Isaac Babel deals with mankind's timeless sufferings and joys, and in his novel *The Red Cavalry* describes love in its most naked form and the physiological ravages of death.

But after 1925, reaction sets in against the modernist tendencies unleashed and given broader scope by the October Revolution. The announcement of the First Five-Year Plan, which supplants the New Economic Policy, is accompanied by a warning to writers in the form of a resolution of the Central Committee. Though this resolution recognizes the distinctive nature of art and literature, it stresses the principle of "social leadership." "Just as the class struggle in general is not yet ended," this resolution states, "so it has not yet ended on the literary front. In the class society there is no neutral art nor can there be any such art, even though the nature of art in general and literature in particular is expressed in forms that are far more divergent than in politics, for example."

The wild, luxuriant growth of the 1920's is brought under strict control in 1932. Once the opposition of the left is eliminated, Stalin and the Communist bureaucracy, of which he is the supreme representative, use the end of the First Five-Year Plan, which in their eyes is the first step toward the building of Socialism in a single country, as a pretext to enlist all Soviet writers beneath the same banner and make them entirely subservient to the Party: the associations of independent writers are dissolved and their members summarily enrolled in the Union of Soviet Writers. Dogmatism then becomes the unbreachable wall circumscribing the realm of writers and making it more and more of an intellectual and artistic prison. The intriguing prospects of a revolutionary literature become a thing of the past. Esthetic judgment becomes subservient to the most primitive sort of Manichaeanism: the pure and simple glorification of Party decisions is accorded the pompous title of Socialist Realism and celebrated as a triumphant new step forward, while the writer who shows the slightest sign of independence, even of the most harmless sort, immediately risks being marked with the infamous brand of "Formalism" by the political powers that be. Not sacrificing form to ideology is henceforth considered an artistic crime.

The end of the era that has been called the bronze age of Revolution destroys those whose genius was its crowning glory. Mayakovsky commits suicide in 1930. Meyerhold, shorn now of all his functions, makes one last appearance at the Congress of Theater Directors in 1939. The Party had hoped to force him back into its ranks after the long penance it had imposed upon him. The speech he delivered on this occasion proved, however, that his loyalties could not be co-opted. "This pitiable and sterile thing that claims to be Socialist Realism," he had the courage to state publicly, "has nothing to do with art. Theater belongs to the realm of art, and without art there is no theater. Go to Moscow theaters and have a look at the dull and boring performances, which differ only in their degree of proximity to absolute worthlessness. . . . In the great circles in which once upon a time there was only fervent and constantly renewed artistic life, in which men devoted to art engaged in research, conducted experiments, lost their way and found new paths for achieving *mises-en-scène* that sometimes were bad and sometimes marvelous, one now finds only a depressing mediocrity, [men] possessed of the greatest good will but overcome with despair and displaying a terrible lack of talent." The day after this explosive speech, Meyerhold is arrested and dies not long after, either as a result of the interrogations he is made to undergo or because he is mistreated in an internment camp. His wife, the famous actress Zinaida Reich, is murdered a few weeks after her husband's arrest.

5

The German Revolutionary Theater

The revolutionary art that flowers after the October Revolution in the Soviet Union tends to spread to other countries simply because of its Socialist aims that recognize no national boundaries. It gains a particularly firm foothold in Germany, for that country is shaken to its foundations by revolutionary movements. Though all of German art is affected by it, it is above all in the theater that attempts are made to apply the new esthetic born in the East during the Weimar Republic. Meyerhold's most faithful and most talented disciples were undoubtedly Erwin Piscator and Bertolt Brecht.

At the beginning of his career in the theater, Piscator's activities were closely modeled on Bogdanov's "Proletkult"; in 1920 he joins with revolutionary groups in founding the "proletarian theater" whose aim is "the conscious accentuation and propagation of the idea of class struggle." Art properly speaking is of no concern; the aim is to "engage in politics," on improvised stages in public meeting halls in the working-class district of Berlin. But just as Lenin and Lunacharsky rebel against the excesses of Bogdanov's

"Proletkult" in the Soviet Union, so the German Communist Party disapproves of an enterprise in which Communist doctrine merely serves as a cloak for revolutionary hopes that have not been examined in the light of reason. The eternal dilemma of Marxism, constantly torn between valuing esthetic pleasure (while admittedly enlisting it in the service of political action) and bald indoctrination that disdains any form of artistic appeal, is reflected in this criticism of proletarian theater by *Red Flag,* the chief organ of the German Communist Party: "One reads in the program . . . that it is not art but propaganda . . . , that the aim is to express on the stage the proletarian and Communist idea for propagandistic and educational purposes. There is not supposed to be any 'esthetic pleasure.' But in that case the word theater should not be used: it should be called by its rightful name—propaganda. The word theater implies art, artistic creation. . . . Art is too sacred a thing for its name to be applied to vulgar propaganda. . . . What the worker needs in our day is a vigorous art . . . it matters little if this art is of bourgeois origin, so long as it is art."

Following the failure of proletarian theater, Piscator goes back to previous experiments, particularly those of Meyerhold, and arrives at conceptions of theater that represent a remarkable application of Marxist esthetics to problems of staging. Piscator develops a highly personal style, and at the same time deals with all the concerns he and his contemporaries share as they search for the right road to Socialism. Piscator's theater thus has a political, an epic, and a technical aspect.

In Piscator's view, the individual no longer exists; heavy

industry and war have made man into a new being possessed of a new sort of subjective life and motivated by the will of his class. That is why the new dramatic art must turn from the individual and his personal and private problems to the destiny of the masses. "Man as shown on the stage," he writes, "is of importance to us because of his social function. It is neither his relationship to himself nor his relationship to God that matter, but rather his relationship to society. When he appears on the stage his class or his rank in society appear with him. When he is caught up in a moral, spiritual, or instinctual conflict, he enters into conflict with society. . . . A period in which the reciprocal relationships of the collectivity, the revision of all human values, the transformation of all social relations have become the order of the day can look at man only from the point of view of his position with regard to the society and the social problems of his time, that is to say as a *political* being."

As an opponent of the dramatic art aimed at Aristotelian catharsis which seeks to arouse our pity by showing the personal misfortunes that may befall a man rather than furthering our sense of rebellion against the social causes of human misery, Piscator turns to an epic form of theater which makes generous use of documents justifying the class struggle and the materials necessary to further the audience's understanding of the mechanisms of society. The three unities of time, place, and action derived from an interpretation of Aristotelian esthetics that was both incorrect and incomplete seem to him to have been outmoded ever since Shakespeare demonstrated that action becomes far more intense and far more interesting if it is presented in an epic style. But it is cinema that dealt classic dramatic art the death blow, for films taught us how to deal successfully with complicated action that unfolds in a number of different time periods and a number of different locales.

The theater must now adopt modern techniques. Just as social and spiritual revolutions are always accompanied by technical changes, so a new art of theater can be developed only if technical innovations in stagecraft become the rule. Apart from the moving platform and electric lighting, the stage has remained almost the same as in Shakespeare's day. It is still a rectangle that enables the spectator to take a "forbidden peek" at a strange world. This conservatism stems from the fact that before 1917 theater had never been in the hands of the oppressed class. Now that the proletariat is coming into power, the moment has come to liberate theater, not only spiritually but structurally.

The internal consistency and the explosive power of Piscator's dramatic esthetic were responsible for its rapid spread even beyond the borders of Germany. From 1928 on, theatrical troupes made up of both amateur and professional actors are formed in many countries and take on the task of propagating Communist ideas in a dramatic form that is highly effective, thanks to Piscator's many experiments. These are the famous "Agit-Prop" (agitation and propaganda) troupes; by 1931 there are three hundred of them in Germany. The "Agit-Prop" program has been summed up in four points by one of the movement's theoreticians: "I. Art is not an end in itself nor is its aim the personal delectation of the individual; II. Art for us is an agitation that arouses the masses and an event that revolutionizes and points to the goal to be pursued; III. Art for us is a collective creation, an intellectual cooperation that feels what the masses feel and embodies the will of the masses; IV. Art to us is a means of demonstrating our class hatred of capitalism and of expressing our determination to arrive at Communism and a classless society. We do not rack our brains to discover what will happen in the centuries to come; we do not bury ourselves in folio volumes to acquaint ourselves with the past history of the theater. We are alive today; it is in the present that we must wage our fight to transform that present by revolution."

Bertolt Brecht's great and exceptional merit lies in his having been able to preserve the revolutionary fervor of his theater long after the revolutionary impetus of theater had died out in the Soviet Union. In a certain sense he is the only Communist writer whose creative genius was not paralyzed by the iron collar of Socialist Realism. This is unquestionable proof of Brecht's enormous adaptability and perhaps proof also of a talent for theater which, far from being snuffed out by exterior constraints, reacts to outside pressures by overcoming its own limitations.

Brecht's esthetics is a continuation of Piscator's, which in turn had been inspired by Meyerhold's. We find in it almost the same constituent elements and the same arguments as in his predecessors. But Brecht has one advantage over them: he is not only a theoretician and a polemicist but also a creative artist. In Brecht's case there is a continual dialectical interplay between Marxist reflection, or at least reflection that is meant to be Marxist, and creative activity that keeps this theorizing from being too abstract. Marxist esthetics, which shares the extreme intellectualism of Marxist doctrine as a whole and thus tends to be very stiff and wooden, takes on an unexpected, unpredictable, almost impulsive quality when Brecht writes on the subject. Marxist esthetics is too often stripped to a bare skeleton, a procedure that is very helpful in anatomical studies but is not at all appropriate for the study of any sort of living reality. In certain characters in Brecht's theater, Mother Courage or Mr. Puntila or Galileo for example, this skeleton is draped in living flesh that palpitates and quivers with sensations and appetites that are usually ignored and condemned by the deadly dull exponents of Socialist puritanism.

The new theater that the Marxist Bertolt Brecht is eager to develop bears the name of "epic theater." The principles governing are set forth most clearly in his *Notes on the Opera Mahagonny* (1931) and his *Little Organon for the Theater* (1949). As with Piscator, the principal characteristics of epic theater stem from a general opposition to traditional theater.

The first difference between traditional theater and epic theater lies in their view of the individual. Traditional theater presents heroes whose character and conscience are what determine their fate, to the exclusion of any outside factor. The classic theater thus makes no distinction between a man and his destiny; they are viewed as being intimately interrelated even before the curtain goes up. Epic theater, by contrast, takes account of the profound gap that technology and bureaucratization, the hegemony of economic powers and the anonymous nature of political power have created between the individual and his environment. Economic and social processes have become so complex that it is impossible for the individual to understand the mechanism behind them and control it. Once a subject, man has now become an object of history. Since it is now impossible to show man as an independent, self-motivated creature whose life is guided by principles he finds within his own conscience, the theater must turn its attention to the totality of forces which seem to be enslaving man. This shift in perspective necessarily calls for a new method of theatrical representation. "Today, when the human being must be thought of as 'the sum total of all social relationships,' the epic form is the only one able to deal with these processes which furnish dramatic art with the raw material for an all-embracing image of the world. Man too, that is to say the flesh and blood man, can be understood only in the light of the processes in which he is involved and through which he exists," Brecht writes.

It is precisely because traditional theater is out of step with the times and therefore does not fulfill its proper social function that its one goal has become sheer entertainment. By contrast with this "epicurianism" which makes pleasure more important than knowledge, and the cult of the beautiful, now shorn of all content whatsoever, more prestigious than the useful, the new theater attempts to arouse and strengthen the spectator's critical faculty, and thus necessarily goads him into taking revolutionary action. "The goal that was sought," Brecht writes of his theatrical reforms, "was a theater appropriate to the century of science, and if it proved too difficult for those who envisioned such a theater to borrow or steal enough from the arsenal of esthetic concepts to be able to defend themselves against the esthetes of the press, they simply threatened to 'transform an enjoyable product into an instrument of education and to turn certain institutions, which were mere pleasure-palaces, into organs for the dissemination of a doctrine.' "

Esthetic pleasure, however, is proscribed only insofar as it becomes an end in itself. It is permissible, and even desirable, when it serves the cause of knowledge. Pleasure and education must go hand in hand. "Theater should not merely be called upon to produce a body of knowledge, images that teach us what reality is like. Our theater must arouse a *fervent desire* to know, and take care to provide the *pleasure* the spectator feels when reality is transformed. Our audiences must not only learn how Prometheus bound is freed of his chains, but also be induced to feel the pleasure that results from his liberation. All the desires and all the pleasures of inventors and discoverers and the feelings of triumph of liberators must be taught by our theater," he writes.

The Brechtian esthetic as embodied in various aspects of epic theater is based on the primacy of being over consciousness: in this sense it is Marxist through and through. This principle underlies Brecht's distinction between a classic theater that explores only consciousness, that makes it the source of being, and an epic theater that brings being front and center in order that consciousness may arrive at a decision after having thoroughly explored it. Whereas classic theater establishes the most intimate ties between action and the morality that results from it, epic theater separates the descriptive element and the didactic element. Whereas classic theater captures the emotional loyalties of the spectator as a result of the illusion that the esthetic element and the ethical element are in complete harmony, epic theater does away with any such feelings by creating a critical attitude dictated by the power of reason and born of the distinction that is established between the reality that it puts before the spectator and the reflections that this reality gives rise to. In classic theater the spectator is caught up in an action that is entirely self-consistent, thanks to the author's careful plotting; in epic theater the spectator witnesses a series of tableaux that are not linked together by any sort of artificial device, thus enabling him to "keep his distance" from the spectacle set before him; he is thus a witness, in a manner of speaking, to a sociological experiment accompanied by a commentary.

Brecht himself drew up a brief outline of the differences between the dramatic form of old-style theater and the epic form of the new theater:

Dramatic form	*Epic form*
Active	Narrative
Involves the spectator in the action on the stage	Transforms the spectator into an observer
Puts an end to his activity	Arouses his activity
Allows him to experience sensations	Forces him to make decisions
Event	Image of the world
The spectator is caught up in something	The spectator is opposed

Suggestion	Argument
Feelings remain the same	Feelings are exacerbated to the point of becoming understanding
The spectator is square in the middle	The spectator stands apart
Participates in the action	Ponders
Man is supposedly a familiar thing	Man is the object of examination
Man is unchangeable	Man is changeable and effects change
Interest is captured by the outcome of the issue	Interest is captured by the march of events
One scene leads to another	Each scene is important in and of itself
Increasing tension	Montage
Linear progression	Spiral progression
Evolutionism	Leaps and bounds
Static man	Man as process
Thinking determines being	Social existence determines thought
Feeling	Relationship

The principles of epic theater are rigorously applied in plays that Brecht describes as "exemplary." The action is reduced to the dimensions of a short "fable," the purpose of which is to illustrate a political lesson. Theater becomes entirely functional; its one purpose is to arouse the consciousness and the revolutionary will of the masses. Brecht's sole aim is to use theater to teach Marxism by exemplifying revolutionary attitudes and above all by showing that these attitudes are the only proper ones. The theater is given over entirely to the proletariat; the mission of the stage is "to teach as it learns."

The primacy of the "totality of social relations" is carried to extreme lengths in this theater, to the point that it becomes a total and unconditional obedience to the idea of Socialist revolution. The disappearance of all individuality that results is particularly illustrated in the *Didactic Play of Baden: On Consent* (1930). Four aviators are questioned by the chorus, that is to say the Party: "Who are you?" And the aviators reply: "We aren't anybody."

This apparent rejection of all subjectivity might have led Brecht to the sort of economic and social fetishism that is the permanent danger of Marxist esthetics. But he continually takes advantage of the antidote which Marxism provides, thereby recovering his balance every time he risks falling into a paralyzing dogmatism: he makes his "didactic theater" the instrument of a very attractive dialectic. The transformation of the world becomes an absolute value for him: the building of a new social system is less important to him than keeping society moving ahead, than tirelessly searching for the truth, than engaging in reflection that is eternally fresh and new. The *Didactic Play of Baden* ends with this proclamation celebrating the endless march onward and upward:

> We agree that everything must be changed
> The world and humanity
> Especially class unrest
> Because there are two sorts of men
> Exploitation and ignorance. . . .
> When you have improved the world

> Improve the improved world
> Leave it behind! . . .
> When in improving the world you have completed the truth
> Complete the completed truth
> Leave it behind! . . .
> When in completing the truth, you have changed humanity
> Change changed humanity
> Leave it behind!

Brecht's esthetic thus proves that a truly Marxist esthetic is at once constraining and liberating. Subservience to political power is necessary in order to put an end to class struggle, but once this stage is past this subservience must end; Marxist dogma furthers the search for truth, but it is not truth itself; Socialism is a higher stage of human society, but not the final stage. In this larger perspective Marxist esthetics is above all the recognition of artistic and literary praxis, that is to say of the creative effort that, by making men aware of their historical situation, inspires them to build Socialism today and doubtless to go beyond it tomorrow.

6

Socialist Realism

"Socialist Realism" is adopted as the official watchword at the First Congress of Soviet Writers in August 1934. At this juncture the phrase does not refer to a special style that the writer is to employ; it is used, rather, as a definition of the artistic principle underlying all works that win the official stamp of approval. It represents, in fact, the decisive victory and the extension to the entire realm of culture of the "Party spirit" (*partignost*) which Lenin first mentioned in his 1905 article "Organization and Party Literature." Regarded in the beginning as one of the basic elements in Marxist esthetics, it becomes the most important element as the regime is consolidated, that is to say as it turns into a rigid and distrustful conservatism. Disguised as literary criticism, Socialist Realism thus represents a bureaucratic and administrative conception of literature notable both for the exceptional vagueness and fuzziness of its notions in the realm of pure esthetics and for the implacable rigor of its judgments, which for the most part have no justification other than the political needs of the moment.

Gorky and Stalin are both hailed as the fathers of Socialist Realism, and it is difficult to determine the precise role played by the two men in its founding. The *Great Soviet Encyclopedia,* every word of which must be approved by the leaders of the Party, gives all the credit to Stalin. "It was by taking as his point of departure the definition of the artistic method of Soviet literature formulated by J. W. Stalin that Gorky developed the fundamental principles of the art of Socialist Realism," the *Encyclopedia* states. On the other hand, *The History of Russian Literature,* a somewhat less official work, attributes the prime role to Gorky. "Thus Gorky discovered the principle or artistic creation which in a conversation with writers J. W. Stalin later defined as the method of Socialist Realism," it states.

With his novel *Mother* and his drama *The Enemies,* works written a year after the Revolution of 1905, Gorky in fact laid down the first solid bases for a genuine Socialist literature. The class struggle is exposed in these works in all its naked brutality: in *The Enemies* in particular the struggle is not so much between individuals as between the oppressive capitalist order and revolutionary masses thirsting for liberation. But the obligatory revision of the cultural policy that the Soviet Union had followed earlier is directly connected with Stalin's 1932 conversation with Gorky and Alexei Tolstoy. In the name of Socialist Realism, a term invented by Stalin himself, the latter sets up rigid rules governing art and literature and declares that now that a scientifically established doctrine is available to Soviet writers, they must consider themselves "engineers of the human soul." Alexei Tolstoy, moreover, sets Russians an example of blind submission to Stalin's will. A former aide-de-camp of Denikin, he has no compunction about celebrating Stalin's exploits at Tsaritsyn, thus humiliating the man who was his military leader during the civil war with all the fervor of the convert and all the convenient forgetfulness of the past of the turncoat.

The course the Congress itself takes is largely determined by Gorky and Zhdanov. In his address to the Congress Gorky deals primarily with one of the major themes of Marxist esthetics, the writer's obligation to see that his literary activity goes hand in hand with the overall activity of society and thus contributes to the struggle that mankind must wage against the constraints imposed upon it by nature. "Socialist Realism," he proclaims, "firmly supports the view of existence as action, as a creation whose aim is the continual development of the most precious individual capabilities of man to ensure his victory over the forces of nature, his health and long life, the great happiness of being able to live on this earth, which in answer to his ever-increasing needs he wishes to make over entirely, into a magnificent home for all mankind united in a single family." He therefore defines Socialist Realism as "the realism of men who transform and rebuild the world."

Zhdanov, on the other hand, assumes the role of spokesman for Stalin's essentially political views, which he proclaims openly at the Congress, thus anticipating the day when he will brutally enforce them on being made the Soviet Union's cultural dictator by the grace of his master. In Zhdanov's eyes, "being an engineer of souls means having one's two feet firmly planted in real life." And this life centers on the class struggle and the building of the classless society through Socialism. "Yes," he states, "our Soviet literature is biased, and we are proud of that fact, for our bias is that we want to free workers and men of the yoke of capitalist slavery."

The statutes adopted at the end of this First Congress of Soviet Writers state, finally, that "Socialist Realism [. . .] demands of the artist a truthful, historically concrete representation of reality in its revolutionary development. Moreover, he must contribute to the ideological transformation and the education of workers in the spirit of Socialism."

It must be noted, however, that despite this clear public expression of the Party's determination to confine literature within an extremely rigid framework and to allow only such works as will further the building of Socialism, a great many speakers, following the example of Marx and Engels, attempt to preserve the cultural heritage of the past by viewing Socialist Realism as the continuation of a progressivist literary tradition rather than a reflection of the current political situation. Louis Aragon thus reminds the Congress that Socialist Realism is the culmination of a literary effort pursued in French literature by Balzac, Zola, Pottier, Vallès, Stendhal, Barbusse, Rimbaud, and Péguy. Johannes R. Becher, who had been an Expressionist poet before becoming a convert to the Marxist esthetic and reverting to a popular lyricism, traces a continuous line of development in German literature from Goethe and Schiller through Weerth, the plebeian and popular nature of whose writings Marx and Engels had praised, and the political poetry of Freiligrath, to Socialist Realism.

This linking of Socialist Realism with the past is never to

be totally condemned. In order to bridge the gap between the past and the present, all that is required is to apply the term "critical realism," which had long been common in Russian literary criticism, to all bourgeois writers whose works seem at all compatible with a Socialist point of view. Thus Socialist Realism can be regarded as merely a higher stage of critical realism; looked at from this point of view, it becomes a permanent principle of esthetics accompanying and illustrating the class struggle throughout human history.

Since Socialist Realism is oriented toward the future, which Party dogma suggests will be a happy one because the class struggle will have ended and nature will have been completely tamed, Marxist esthetics, in line with this new policy, regards it as a right, and indeed a duty, to say yes to life. Socialist Realism thus is basically optimistic: it is different in this respect from critical realism, the exponents of which had a clear view of the problems of their time and were well aware of how tragically serious they were, but saw no solution to them and therefore often could not help but have a negative or at least a passive attitude toward life.

Despite the pronounced anti-Romanticism implied by the notion of realism, the revolutionary art of the 1920's is not rejected out of hand, at least in theory. The Congress sides with Gorky's view that the "revolutionary Romanticism" of many writers in the first years of the Revolution was "only a pseudonym for Socialist Realism."

The new canons of an esthetic that transforms writers into "engineers of souls" reduces the best of them to silence.

Boris Pilnyac, whose work *The Naked Year* (1922), written in a harsh, staccato language full of syntactical surprises, had been a powerful portrayal of individuals struggling against the fatal mishaps of everyday life; Isaac Babel, who had celebrated the bloody exploits of the Red Cavalry and the ritual fights of the Jewish ruffians of Odessa; Yury Olesha, whose *Envy* (1927) shifts back and forth from the real to the fantastic, all fall silent. Having written works counterpointing the chaos and the enthusiasm of the age, the rebellion, the instability, the eternal questioning and counterquestioning—having captured, in short, the revolutionary spirit in its pure state—these authors cannot resign themselves to the subordination to the narrowly circumscribed ends of the moment that is demanded of them.

An exception should perhaps be made in the case of Sholokhov, even though his second novel, *Virgin Soil Upturned,* was not published until many years after his first, *And Quiet Flows the Don*. This second novel fulfills the essential objectives of Socialist Realism, if not in a wholly convincing manner, at least with an unquestionable talent that does not appear to have been too severely crippled by the limitations placed upon it. The theme of this novel is the collectivization of the land and the human reactions to this profound transformation of society. Though Sholokhov resorts to a certain typology based on class differences, he manages to avoid the artificiality that such typing on the basis of class often leads to, and all his characters are three-dimensional human beings. The main characters in this work which starts out as a mere illustration of measures promulgated by Stalin are real flesh-and-blood people in the

SOCIALIST REALISM

end: Davidov, a Communist worker who is trying to change the Cossacks' instinctive inclinations and make them give up their petty-bourgeois habits, Nagulnov, whose leftist deviationism makes him act counter to the policy of the Communist Party, the kulak Ostrovnov, who joins the collective farm and eventually becomes head of it but nonetheless cannot rid himself of his class mentality.

But for most men of letters who continue to write, among them Fedin, Leonov, and Katayev, Socialist Realism is a terrible hindrance, and in order to work at all they are forced to sacrifice their talent and their own inspiration as creative writers. As for literary form, the political content forced upon it becomes a more and more crushing burden. Kept in the strictest subservience to politics, it undergoes a sort of decline, becoming little more than a collection of recipes and tricks that students may learn at the Gorky Institute of Literature in Moscow.

As for what little is left of "revolutionary Romanticism" in an increasingly bureaucratic society, it eventually degenerates into a kind of technique of cheap illustration mindful of the nineteenth-century Epinal prints for popular consumption. Kolkhoz novels hail the virtues of collective effort, Stakhanovism and its production quotas are depicted in the most glowing colors, the defense of the Soviet Union against the imperialist dragon takes on the proportions of a holy crusade, Stalin's genius is celebrated as though he were the godhead itself. Zhdanov, Stalin's right-hand man, is made the guiding light and the grand inquisitor of this didactic realism.

Because Socialist Realism demands that the writer be

absolutely loyal to the Socialist ideal, the heroes of his works must be "positive." In Russian literature in the great tradition, there were admittedly only "negative" heroes, madmen, idiots, fatalistic skeptics, or dreamy-eyed idlers, in short people who were social outsiders. But according to the doctrinaires of Socialist Realism, Russian authors had chosen to write about such characters precisely because they had only hatred or scorn for the society in which they lived. Literature therefore offered images that rejected or challenged the established order. The Soviet writer, however, presumably loves his society; he thus has a different view of his role than did his predecessors and when he looks around him he will naturally be most inspired by the "positive" values that society has to offer.

The hero in Soviet literature must be "positive" chiefly because of the supposed absence of conflict in the new society. The principal resource of the bourgeois novel and drama was an interesting plot. Crimes, adventures, questions of money, adultery, in short all the patterns of a decadent and rotten world were what kept it moving. But these plot devices are not appropriate in a literature whose mission is to reflect and contribute to the advancement of a society that has rid itself of all the vices inherent in the bourgeois social order. That is why Socialist Realism replaces the decadent complexities of an involved plot with the ponderous simplicities of a soul-stirring subject. Need we add that the application of this principle, namely the elimination of any sort of plot, vastly impoverishes the characters? Placed in an aseptic universe they become thin and insubstantial, and serve only as sketchy illustrations of a sententious moralism.

The 1945 victory over the Fascism that was a product of the Western world, a triumph that cost the Soviet Union dearly, reinforces the characteristically Russian tendencies of Socialist Realism. The policy of fervently celebrating the superiority of the Russian creative genius goes hand in hand with a struggle against any sort of foreign influence, against the constant temptation of corruption that the Party labels "cosmopolitanism" and continually denounces. The encyclical promulgated by the Central Committee of the Communist Party of the Soviet Union on August 14, 1946, states that Soviet culture is better than any other culture because Soviet writers have become aware of the rationale behind Party strictures against apolitical literature and have declared war on estheticism. "The strength of Soviet literature, which is the most advanced literature in the world, lies in the fact that it is a literature which has and can have no other interests than the interests of the people, the interests of the State. The function of Soviet literature is to aid the State in properly educating young people, in answering their needs, in teaching the new generation to be strong. That is why everything that tends to foster an absence of ideology, apoliticalism, 'Art for Art's sake' is foreign to Soviet literature and is harmful to the interests of the people and the Soviet State," it reads.

"Zhdanovism," which after 1946 is more or less synonymous with Socialist Realism, acquires its distinctive character by accentuating this postwar chauvinism. "Our literature," Zhdanov writes in his book *On the Subject of Art and Science,* published in 1951, "is the youngest of all the literatures of all peoples and all countries. At the same time it is the literature that is the richest in ideas, the most progressive, and the most revolutionary. . . . Only Soviet literature, which is of the same flesh and blood as our building of Socialism, could be such a progressive, intellectually fertile, and revolutionary literature."

The pressure brought to bear against writers, who are reduced by Zhdanovism to the role of docile bystanders explicating the political decisions of the Central Committee and Party satraps, becomes stronger and stronger. The mishaps that befall the novelist Fadeyev are proof of this. In 1946 Fadeyev wins the Stalin Prize for his novel *The Young Guard*. Despite this official recognition, which is also a reward for his services as the secretary of the Union of Soviet Writers, the Party press criticizes the novel for not sufficiently stressing "the role of the Party as a guide and an educator." Fadeyev finds himself obliged to rewrite his novel. *Pravda,* which had violently attacked him, is then pleased to note that as a result of his revision "the educational value of the work has been considerably enhanced, for young people in particular." Following this recantation that he has forced himself to make, Fadeyev gives up all literary activity and commits suicide in 1956.

During these dark days of Zhdanovism, one of the very few Marxists to speak out against this propagandistic literature trapped in the stifling cage of an official political doctrine and a series of monotonous cliches is George Lukacs. In a book entitled *The Hinge of Fate,* he bases his criticism of Soviet literature under the dictatorship of Socialist Realism on the famous law of uneven development whose Marxist orthodoxy cannot be questioned. But he applies this law by standing it on its head. Taking precisely the opposite view from Marx and Engels, Lukacs maintains that it is cultural evolution that lags behind economic evolution rather than vice-versa. According to Lukacs, the stagnation of Soviet literature is totally at odds with the enormous expansion of the Soviet economy. "On the one hand, the immense strides made by the Socialist economy, the rapid extension of proletarian democracy, the emergence of great numbers of dynamic personalities from the masses and the growth of proletarian humanism in the praxis of workers and their leaders are having an important and revolutionary influence on the consciousness of the most outstanding intellectuals of the capitalist world. Conversely, we are witness to the fact that our Soviet literature has not yet gone beyond the lingering traditions of the decadent bourgeoisie that stand in the way of its development," he writes.

But immediately thereafter, George Lukacs is obliged to retract his statement, and in a most humiliating way moreover, for he is forced to attribute what he now describes as his errors of judgment to his lack of familiarity with Soviet literature. "Since it would seem that I was not sufficiently prepared to speak of Soviet literature in an essay of a scientific nature . . . I should have limited myself to dealing with certain Soviet writers in more modest, more unpretentious studies, or in simple reader's notes. In spite of my backwardness, I hope to correct my errors . . ." But since he is also a clever tactician, Lukacs then attempts to excuse his former frankness by alluding to one of the fundamental principles of dialectical materialism, the intimate relationship between form and content. Just as the evolution of the forces of production brings about a modification of the relations of production, so the change of political and social content that has taken place in the Soviet Union will necessarily eventually give rise to a form that will be an adequate expression of that content. The installation of a Socialist regime will give birth to "a higher level of style in the history of literature."

Having been enthroned by a political regime that had every intention of using it to serve its own purposes in whatever way it pleased, Socialist Realism comes under fire the moment it becomes evident that a change in the political climate has taken place in the Soviet Union. The death of Stalin is of course the turning point marking the passage from Jacobin Terror to a Directorate, or in the terms used by the Party, from the cult of personality to collective leadership. But however strange it may seem, there were evidences of this change of direction as early as 1952, when Stalin was still in power, and what is more, it was Stalin himself who pointed it out. In his famous article "Marxism and Questions of Language," which we have already mentioned, Stalin denies "the class nature of language" and regards it as playing no part in the ideological superstructure. Using this initial concession as support for its views, the Moscow Institute of Philosophy, under the direction of G. F. Alexandrov, seeks to limit the dimensions of the ideological superstructure even further. This liberation of certain sectors of cultural life is undertaken with particular fervor since Alexandrov himself had been violently attacked by Zhdanov for having stressed in his *History of Western Philosophy* the major role Western thought played in the origins of Marxism.

The first disciplines to become independent of ideology are formal logic, mathematics, and the natural sciences. As for art and literature, opinions differ. Some theoreticians agree entirely with Marx and Engels, who had unhesitatingly assigned art a more or less absolute value in and of itself; others follow Lenin, who had wanted cultural activity to be first and foremost a powerful weapon in the class struggle. Little by little a compromise is arrived at: while it is part of ideology, and therefore has political functions to perform, art is quite different from other forms of ideology, such as philosophy, political propaganda, and so on.

The argument comes to a head during the Nineteenth Congress of the Communist Party of the Soviet Union in October 1952, when Malenkov, who has succeeded Zhdanov, attacks the latter's entire policy without mentioning him by name. He particularly criticizes the "varnishing over of realities," the dull and tiresome optimism, and the bland stupidity of Soviet literature, which has been obliged to present only "positive" heroes and to tone down any real "conflicts." The Soviet writer in his view contributes to the building of Socialism not by writing fervent dithyrambs praising it but by having the courage to stress its imperfections. "What we need are Soviet Gogols and Shchedrins, who use burning satire to root out from life everything that is negative, fusty, and out of date, everything that stands in the way of our march onward," Malenkov cries.

The death of Stalin in 1953 brings on the famous "thaw," the most important manifestations of which are Ehrenburg's *The Thaw* (1954), Dudintsev's *Not by Bread Alone* (1956), and Galina Nikolayeva's *Battle on the Way*. But even though these works denounce the misdeeds of Stalinism rather than praising its benefits, the Marxist esthetics deformed by twenty years of Socialist Realism shows few signs of change. It still gives evidence of the same absence of any sort of search for new techniques, the same mechanical rhythms, in short the same sort of scorn for form as before. The absolute primacy of political and social content remains unchallenged.

The Second Congress of Soviet Writers in 1954 would appear to be a step backward if measured against the declaration of Malenkov, who as a matter of fact had just been replaced by Alexandrov as Minister of Culture. Thus the report of this Congress in the second part of the collective work entitled *The Soviet Union Academy of Sciences History of Soviet Literature* places particular emphasis on the inalienable loyalty of writers to the Party: "All the writers who addressed the Congress unanimously declared that they regarded the leadership of the Party as the guarantee of their success and rejected the deceptive bourgeois 'slogan' of 'the independence of literature within society' in favor of the Leninist concept of the *partignost* of literature, enrolled in the service of the interests of the people."

Thus a guideline for post-Stalinian art and literature gradually emerges. Zhdanovism, with its ridiculous push-button optimism and its overt meddling dictated by a petty, narrow-minded distrust, is abandoned. But instead of restoring to Marxist esthetics the dialectical breadth and the boundless receptivity that it had had in classical Marxism, theorists are content with a "Leninist renaissance."

Following the Twentieth Congress of the Communist Party of the Soviet Union in 1956 which makes de-Stalinization official, an editorial in the Party organ *The Communist* attests to the effort to outline an entirely new policy. The firm determination to combat Stalinist arteriosclerosis is evidenced by the attention paid to the infinite variety of forms that literary activity may assume. Past, present, and future experiments in literary form meet with more or less total approval. This very liberal esthetics is Marxist in character principally because it encourages creative subjectivity rather than condemning it as in the Stalinist era. "A fundamental condition for the development of a literature and an art that are borne on the wings of lofty ideas and are truly artistic is the unremitting struggle against uniformity and a reduction to the lowest common denominator in artistic creation. Only a vigorous and expressive art can satisfy the esthetic needs of Soviet citizens and fulfill its function as an active tool of education. The task of Soviet writers and artists lies in their appropriating for the domain of artistic mastery all the wealth that humanity has accumulated and boldly adding to this wealth by new creative discoveries. Socialist Realism sets no limits in this respect. It presupposes a variety of styles and forms of artistic creation, and also a variety of methods of depicting the typical."

But if we examine the freedom thus granted and recommended more closely, we see that it concerns only form, and therefore must be regarded as a half measure. More importantly, it is a dubious one if we accept the strict Marxist principle that there is a necessary relationship between form and content. Once form is freed of constraint, the content should likewise be freed of its confining social and political limitations. Though that is the hope of the younger generation of Soviet writers, which in the long run will prove to be irrepressible, the Party nonetheless continues to zealously maintain its dictatorial grip on literature. Thus when the Third Congress of Soviet Writers meets in 1959, the Central Committee reminds those present that "the duty of Soviet writers is to provide a true and lifelike demonstration of the beauty of the exploits of the people at work [. . .] to be the fervent exponents of the Seven-Year Plan and to breathe courage and energy into the hearts of Soviet citizens."

Any sort of real liberalization of Soviet literature becomes impossible, moreover, by the very fact that the cultural bureaucracy created by Stalinism, and still faithful to its spirit, remains unchallenged. The constraint exercised on writers is twofold. Firstly, an enormous bureaucratic mechanism made up of study committees and investigatory committees, of committees that lay down guidelines and committees on policy, all of which control the publication of literary works, more or less eats up the writer's time, dictates what is to inspire him, and reduces his talent to the lowest common denominator. "Many Soviet writers," Solzhenitsyn writes in a letter to the Fourth Congress of Soviet Writers (1967), "have changed chapters, pages, paragraphs, and sentences in their works; they have toned them down merely to ensure that they would be printed and have thus ruined them beyond redemption." This bureaucracy, secondly, is fiercely opposed to any attempt to shed light on the deep underlying causes of Stalinism and to any criticism of the consequences of the regime which placed it in power and which it continues to represent. This "new class" has of course done away with official censorship, but, by more or less covertly exercising a censorship that favors its interests, has made it even more irksome, for its workings are now impossible to understand. This is what has led Lukacs to complain in the most bitter terms in his *Problems of Realism* that the spirit of Stalinism has not really been done away with. "The main problem of Socialist Realism today," he states, "is the critical elimination of the Stalinist era. This is of course the principal task confronting Socialist ideology as a whole. I shall here concern myself only with the realm of literature. If Socialist Realism, which as a consequence of the Stalinist era at times became a humiliating insult even in Socialist countries, is eager to attain the same high level that it enjoyed in the 1920's, it must once again take to the highroad that enables it to portray contemporary man as he really is. And this highroad necessarily leads by way of a faithful description of the Stalinist decades in all their inhumanity."

He continues: "Sectarian bureaucrats are opposed to this, claiming that it is necessary to bury the past and deal only with the present situation, Stalinism being a phase of history that has now come to an end, that has disappeared. Such a statement is not only false—the way it is phrased is clear proof by itself that an extremely influential Stalinist bureaucracy still exists—but also totally meaningless."

7

Bertolt Brecht and George Lukacs

Marxist esthetics has been the subject of two very revealing debates separated by almost a century. The first of these takes place in 1858 between Marx and Engels, on the one side, and Ferdinand Lassalle on the other, on the subject of the latter's play *Franz von Sickingen*. The second takes place between the two greatest theoreticians of Socialist Realism, Bertolt Brecht and George Lukacs, who cross swords three times, in 1932, 1938, and 1966, this latter date being that of the almost simultaneous publication of Lukacs' *Esthetics* in two volumes and of Brecht's posthumous *Writings on Literature and Art* in three volumes, which for the first time brings together all the texts of their discussion.

Having fallen in the bad graces of the Party on publication of his *History and Class Consciousness* in 1923, George Lukacs turns to literary criticism. But he does not thereby cease to be interested in politics; rather, he carries his political concerns over into the area of literature, a tactic in strict conformity with the tenets of Marxist esthetics. With the rising tide of Fascism in Europe, the very fate of Socialism hangs in the balance. Fascism is so powerful that apparently only the concerted efforts of all men who refuse to allow the world to sink into barbarism will be capable of halting its rapid spread. The idea of a popular front uniting the forces of democracy and the forces of Socialism for the defense of progress and civilization begins to take root in the minds of a great number of Communists.

It is precisely this common action of the forces of democracy and the forces of Socialism that Lukacs is attempting to bring about in the area of literature. His plan is to enlist the great bourgeois novelists in the battle against Fascism by freeing them of the reactionary interpretations of which they have been victims and bringing to light their natural tendencies toward critical realism, that is to say the penetrating view of bourgeois society characteristic of them that will necessarily lead to the vision of another society freed of the vices they denounce so fervently, or in other words a classless society. He particularly stresses how important a cultural heritage is to the proletariat. In an article published in the German Communist review *Linkskurve* in 1932, entitled "Let Us Make a Virtue of Necessity," he outlines his future work program, the aim of which is the creation of a genuine Marxist esthetic: "This heritage—accumulated unconsciously—is much greater than it is ordinarily believed to be. In order to unearth this heritage, we would admittedly need a detailed Marxist investigation of three equally important areas, literature, literary theory, and the philosophy of the last fifty or sixty years, and as yet we have not even laid the groundwork for such a study."

This need he feels to forge ties between the traditional heritage and the fight against Fascism inspires Lukacs to write a severe critique of the proletarian literature of the Weimar Republic. A blind faith in the class struggle as the one and only effective weapon, Lukacs warns, leads to a sectarianism that is contrary to the notion of a popular front, for it condemns the bourgeoisie altogether and consigns its literature to the rubbish heap. The critique of the Communist writer Ernst Ottwalt's novel *For They Know What They Do* (1931), which Lukacs writes in 1932 for the review *Linkskurve,* contains a broad outline of the open Marxist esthetic he is endeavoring to create.

According to Lukacs, a modern author must choose between two alternatives: reportage or fictional representation (*Gestaltung*). Ottwalt has chosen the first technique. "Ottwalt's new novel," Lukacs writes, "is representative of a widespread literary orientation, of a specific type of creative method. He employs journalistic techniques rather than the traditional, old-fashioned, bourgeois devices of an invented plot and imaginary characters. This trend is international today: all sorts of writers, from Upton Sinclair and Tretiakov to Ilya Ehrenburg, use this method."

Reportage represents a reaction against the narrowing of the scope of investigation characteristic of contemporary literature. In the face of a reality that seems chaotic, confronted with a life that has no goal or direction, authors turn their backs on the problems of the bourgeois capitalist era and retreat to the dense thickets of the soul, the exploration of which becomes their one concern. The psychologism that results preaches either a capitulation to old ideologies—

the attitude adopted by Dostoevsky, Bourget, and Huysmans—or resignation and indifference toward life in the outside world—the position taken by Hamsun and Anatole France in his early years.

To counteract this flight from the real, reportage stresses the social content, revealing its defects and injustices. It goes too far in the opposite direction however. As objective reality independent of individuals is brought to the fore, the subjective and personal destiny of men is relegated to the background. If psychologism sins by making the human soul its one and only concern, reportage commits an equally grave error when it hypostasizes the social body.

In both cases, the conflict between the subjective and the objective is misrepresented because it is viewed mechanistically rather than dialectically. Both reportage and psychologism reflect the writer's inability, stemming in most cases from a petty-bourgeois mentality, to find his way to the vast areas of human relations that lie behind the objects of social life, to dig down and discover the real nature of the fetishism that characterizes the capitalist system. While psychologistic writers fall into the trap of a subjective idealism, writers who resort to reportage revert to the mechanistic stage of materialism. It matters very little, moreover, which of these two sides of the scale weighs heaviest in an author's work. To separate the objective factors, that is to say social and economic reality, from subjective factors, that is to say the men who create this social and economic reality, is to violate the wholeness of human life in some way or other. The absence of dialectical relations between subjectivity and objectivity causes the former to become merely a moralistic commentary superimposed upon the reportage, while the latter, having been cut loose from its real base, is cast adrift and turns into formalism.

As for the esthetic pleasure that proletarian literature sacrifices the better to fulfill its political role, Lukacs offers the timely reminder that Marx himself was interested in works of art in and of themselves, that he particularly admired the art of antiquity and pondered why classic works continue to "offer us esthetic pleasure and in a certain sense appear to be norms and matchless models."

At this point Lukacs turns to a criticism of Bertolt Brecht's esthetic views. The political activism that Ottwalt sets over and against pure enjoyment, which is essentially bourgeois, seems to Lukacs to bear a close resemblance to Brecht's anti-Aristotelianism, that is to say his anti-classicism. "It corresponds exactly to the contrast Bertolt Brecht establishes between the old theater and the new theater," Lukacs writes. "The former 'allows the spectator to feel, to live the drama, the spectator is caught up in something,' the latter 'forces him to decide,' presents an 'image of the world,' the spectator is 'opposed.' In short, the new art represents a radical break with everything that is old."

In order to rouse the spectator from his passivity, to make him a partner in the transformation of the world, Brecht uses the "alienation effect"; he separates the spectator from the reality being put before him on the stage by surprising him in some way. Lukacs considers this procedure too to be an unjustified severing of dialectical relations. Like those writers who resort to journalistic techniques, Brecht's use of the alienation effect, according to Lukacs, is tantamount to viewing the social content apart from its dialectical relationship with its human substratum. "Since these contents [*i.e.,* the contents of the proletarian Revolution], despite a praiseworthy attempt to make them concrete, remain abstract, that is to say immediate surface phenomena, and since they are not the objective motive forces of the Revolution, their revolutionary spirit also remains an abstract sermon, a 'tendency.' We need only think of Brecht's *The Measures Taken,* wherein the Party's strategic and tactical problems have been reduced to 'ethical problems,' " Lukacs writes.

The real confrontation between Lukacs and Brecht takes place in 1938 in the course of a debate on expressionism they wage in the columns of *Das Wort,* a review founded by Germans in exile. The two antagonists are both eager to fight Fascism. Yet their conceptions of Socialist Realism, which by then has been the official esthetic of the Communist Party for four years, are quite different. Lukacs, who is seeking to bring about a rapprochement with the liberal bourgeoisie in order to make it an ally of the revolutionary proletariat in the fight against Fascism, describes Socialist Realism as a further development of the critical realism of the bourgeois writers of the nineteenth century. Brecht, on the other hand, is convinced that only a radical break with the decadent bourgeoisie will enable the proletariat to win the battle against Fascism, and therefore flatly condemns the whole of bourgeois literature.

In Brecht's view the aim of a literary work is not the esthetic passivity fostered by bourgeois literature, but revolutionary fervor; the awareness of the historical situation created by the work of literature supports and justifies the effort to liberate mankind. Individual freedom of interpretation must therefore give way to the larger freedom that is synonymous with that of all mankind, a freedom that grows continually as all humanity labors to transform the world. That is why Lukacs' literary criticism, insofar as it moves in a particular sphere which is precisely that of purely esthetic contemplation, seems suspect to Brecht. "It is the evidences of capitulation, of retreat from the fray," Brecht writes, "the utopian and idealistic element that one always finds in Lukacs' essays (and that he will surely outgrow) which makes his works unsatisfactory, despite the great number of interesting things in them, and gives one the impression that the only thing that matters to him is enjoyment, not the struggle, the way out, the advance."

This absolute duty of the author to aid in the political struggle is the raison d'être of Brecht's anti-Aristotelian theater, that is to say a theater that rejects any sort of mimetic effect, and far from anesthetizing the spectator's mind and heart, keeps him at a distance in order to allow him to think clearly as he watches the performance and wring from him not cathartic tears but decisions whose effect will be felt after he has left the theater.

In a letter to Willi Bredel, the co-editor of the review *Das Wort,* Brecht complains that Lukacs has classed him with the decadent writers for having used certain literary devices invented by Joyce, Kafka, and Döblin. Brecht does not believe that he has been unfaithful to Marxist esthetics by incorporating new forms within it. In his view the bourgeois novelists of the twentieth century who come to grips with capitalist realities reveal the living forces of our era, even though they may pretend to ignore these realities. Born of contemporary needs and aspirations, their literary techniques are not indissolubly linked to any one specific economic system; they can be used to serve any cause. "Every possible objection to narrative techniques such as montage, interior monologue, or the alienation effect can be raised," Brecht writes, "but it is impossible to object to them from the standpoint of realism, unless we are willing to accept a purely formalist definition of that term. Obviously there can be a kind of interior monologue that may be quite rightly described as formalist, but there are also forms of interior monologue that are realist, and there is no question that one can represent the world of labor with the same exactitude with the aid of montage. In questions concerning pure forms, one must not spout nonsense in the name of Marxism; that is not Marxist."

But the formalism that Lukacs so thoroughly despises would seem to consist rather of seeking to judge literary creation according to criteria based on works of a bygone era, that is to say of attempting to drum into writers' heads a lesson that is no longer of any value to them. Brecht accuses Lukacs of being a pedantic critic, however: "Lukacs recommends to writers: be like Tolstoy, but without his weaknesses; be like Balzac, but be of your own time." To Brecht's way of thinking, these two recommendations are obviously self-contradictory.

To Brecht the real danger inherent in "formalism" is the tendency to cling to outmoded and sclerosed forms. "When certain people see new forms, they scream 'formalism,' but it is they themselves who are the worst formalists, worshipers of old forms at all costs, people who look only at forms, who pay attention to nothing else, who make them the only object of their scrutiny," Brecht writes, referring to Lukacs' antiformalist campaign.

Certain myths created by Lukacs in order to make Socialist Realism appear to be the continuation of a long literary tradition seem to Brecht to be, if not actually false, at least highly suspect. Whereas Lukacs considers Balzac to be the principal representative of critical realism in the nineteenth century, Brecht pretends to see in him nothing but an author of cheap potboilers. The struggles that the individual wages against the entire social order in Balzac's novels remind Brecht not so much of the class struggle as of James Fenimore Cooper's Indian tales, which Balzac himself rather ingenuously admitted having taken as a model. As for Thomas Mann, whom Lukacs regards as the most perfect exemplar of twentieth-century critical realism, Brecht consigns him to literary limbo: "Don't ask me to try to understand *The Magic Mountain* (I am singling Mann out only because he is the epitome of the parvenu bourgeois producer, the author of artificial, pointless, useless books). I frankly confess that I would be willing to make financial sacrifices if it would enable me to prevent the publication of certain books."

The debate, finally, touches on the general problems of literary criticism. Brecht is opposed to any sort of artificial separation of the literary work and criticism. Subjective creativity cannot be made to conform to norms the critic attempts to impose on it from outside. Art obeys only its own laws. "It is wrong to develop a criticism that regards itself as a subject confronting an object, a legislative power for which art provides the executive power," he writes. Criticism must be immanent to the work of art; its cornerstone must be the work of art itself. "However independent art may be, the regulating mechanism (criticism) must be contained within it. It must keep the lines of communication open, it must give the watchword, and so on."

This defense of freedom of execution as indispensable to the work of art is part of a larger campaign Brecht wages to free art and literature of any sort of political interference. His fight against coercive literary criticism is only one aspect of his unyielding opposition to the cultural bureaucracy created by Zhdanov. In his writings we find statements whose form alone makes his deep-rooted hostility toward the bureaucratic mentality crystal-clear: it is sovereign satire settling accounts with the dull-wittedness and the monumental stupidity of the new ruling class. "Art is not capable of turning artistic ideas dreamed up in offices into works of art," Brecht declares categorically. "Only boots can be made to measure. Moreover, the taste of many people who are highly educated from the political point of view is perverted and therefore of no importance whatsoever." Or again, apropos of state planning applied to cultural activities, the attempt in other words to transform writers into "engineers of the soul": "It is not the business of the Marxist-Leninist Party to organize poetic production the way it would set up a chicken farm. If it does so, poems will all be as much alike as one egg is like another."

In the two volumes of his *Esthetics* published in 1966, Lukacs resumes his criticism of Brecht's esthetic views. His critique here is much more subtle and low-keyed than in his earlier writings. He now recognizes Brecht's genius; he confesses, moreover, that he first became acquainted with his great plays only after World War II. The discussion itself is still centered on the three great themes of Brecht's esthetics, scientific theater, the alienation effect, and the problem of the avant-garde.

Following the lead of science, in which experimentation and observation go hand in hand, scientific theater according to Brecht must subject its characters to rigorous experiments by making them come to grips with a reality teeming with contradictions and rent with conflict. By thus confronting the spectator with the real problems of a world that art has not tidied up by giving it an artificial unity, scientific theater forces him to face his responsibilities. Once the theatrical performance has revealed the intimate workings of the alienated world in which he lives and suffers, it is incumbent upon the spectator to intervene in the evolution of history by repairing, so to speak, the mechanism whose structural defects have been pointed out to him.

Lukacs, however, feels that a scientific conception of art disturbs the extremely important relationships between form and content that Marxist dialectics reveals. In science, content is all that matters, since it assigns form a negligible role. But what is worse, Brecht fails to recognize the fundamental difference between the scientific reflection of reality and the artistic reflection, and has thus failed to see the importance of the imaginary in art.

Lukacs' discussion of the alienation effect takes as its point of departure one of Brecht's statements: "The alienation effect enables the spectator to recognize the object, but at the same time it leads him to view it as something strange." For Lukacs, this is a theatrical technique that is improperly superimposed on the play itself. The spectator's interest in a performance should not be dependent on a device artificially laid over the theme of the work being presented like a varnish; it should be a function of the theme itself and the dramatic tensions it embodies. Drama has always managed to surprise and even shock theater audiences by stressing the explosive tensions inherent in the social situation being dealt with. Chekhov, for instance, dramatizes the conflict between the subjective intentions of his heroes and their objective situation. Though he understands the feelings of the characters, which he usually shares, the spectator nonetheless is intensely aware of the conflict between the characters' subjective emotions, for which he feels a profound sympathy, and the objective nature of reality whose preponderant influence he recognizes. "We might say," Lukacs writes, "that all of theater is based on one and the same alienation effect, but precisely for that reason what we witness is drama and not a simple alienation effect."

Whatever reservations he may have expressed with regard to Brecht's esthetics, Lukacs now frees him of the charge of decadence he had brought against him in 1938. He no longer includes him among that avant-garde he accuses of portraying the human being in total isolation rather than showing him in a social framework, of making man's burden heavier through this "dereliction" that is nothing other than "the blind and panic terror of reality." In the beginning Brecht admittedly uses the alienation effect principally as an esthetic device to deny and blot out reality. But the allegories that result from this are not simply the reflection of a subjectivist Nothingness, but on the contrary the embodiment of a revolutionary fervor whose one fault is that it disregards all historical considerations, and thus is too readily persuaded of the imminent collapse of capitalist society. But as Brecht matures, he becomes less inclined to deal with reality in this way that is so out of keeping with historical materialism. Brecht progressively learns to reduce to reasonable proportions this sort of self-hypnotism that Lukacs frequently calls "revolutionary Romanticism."

This evolution of Brechtian esthetics strikes Lukacs as being all the more remarkable in that it did not take place in other arts. Lukacs mentions modern painting, for instance, whose realistic tendencies came to an end with Cézanne and Van Gogh, for great talents such as Matisse and great creators like Picasso never progressed beyond the experimental stage.

Conclusion

Marxist esthetics develops out of Hegelian esthetics, which was centered on problems of content. As an esthetic based on content, it thus manages to avoid two pitfalls that modern esthetics has frequently fallen into: formalism, which consists of reducing art to the formal relationships within the work, that is to say to studying its tone, its symmetry, its rhythm, its style, and so on; and psychologism, which abandons the analysis of the beautiful and instead concerns itself with the subjective pleasure that the beautiful produces.

In Hegelian esthetics the content of art reflects the Idea. Once it has transformed the Hegelian Idea into a social entity, Marxist esthetics is in constant danger of succumbing to the temptations of a simplistic sociologism. This sort of sociologism offers lazy minds a handy prefabricated system of interpretation. It is relatively easy to explain and judge a work of art in terms of the social experience of its author and the esthetic norms adopted by a given society. But the value of the work of art in and of itself is thereby conjured away, a tendency that is exacerbated by the fact that the internationalism of Marxism has made it peculiarly blind to national, geographic, and racial factors, that is to say to everything that cannot be easily fitted into an exclusively economic framework, and has ignored or at least badly neglected the constants and the permanent lines of force created by these factors. Mechanistic Marxism has often rightfully been taxed with being dully simplistic and ridiculously self-complacent, and the same charge might be leveled against a reductive Marxist esthetics, with even more justification perhaps, in that what such an esthetics undermines is the imaginary, an even more delicate and more elusive object than social reality.

Marxist esthetics is equipped, however, to ward off this constant danger. Just as true Marxism cannot be reduced to a simple economic and social view of reality but rather is a global vision that seeks to encompass the entire field of human reality, so true Marxist esthetics in no respect resembles a simple sociology of art; it too aims at totality. In its effort to overlook nothing, to bring together all the elements that comprise the realm of art, it is the exact opposite of a repressive sociologism. The guiding principle of its investigations, namely a living, ongoing, open-ended dialectic, is precisely what makes this esthetic truly Marxist.

It is this principle, hostile to any sort of dogmatism, that causes it to view the complex relations between the work of art and reality as a fruitful and dynamic interaction: relations between form and content, troubled at times by the contradictions of social life, harmonious at times in a society that has solved its contradictions; relations between creative subjectivity and social objectivity, the predominance of the former, thanks to the creative artist's clear vision of the future, alternating with the overriding importance of the latter when thought lags behind economic evolution; relationships between the historicity of artistic creation itself and the suprahistorical value of the created work. Far from freezing the work of art in a definite mold and a definite pattern, dialectics considers every work of art as unfinished; it speaks of it only in terms of eternal becoming, history, resurgence.

Does this mean that dialectics condemns Marxist esthetics to total relativism? The idea of the beautiful and that of esthetic enjoyment admittedly are no longer as absolute and as normative in this esthetic as they are in classic esthetics. But by the very fact that the dialectic of human reality is based on human praxis, that is to say on the creation of man by man, art, being a part of this human reality, both reflects its ceaseless transformations and shares its permanent underlying characteristics. Art participates in the activity of the real, by penetrating to its heart and quickening it through the imaginary.

Marxist esthetics in our century has had two different, and indeed contrary, aspects. The seething, multiform revolutionary art of the 1920's, enriched by all the experiments of Cubism, Expressionism, and Surrealism, was followed by the dull uniformity and exasperating conformism of Socialist Realism. There were inescapable reasons why this was so however. Revolutionary hope is a powerful motive force: renewed and sustained by this fervent and heroic revolutionary spirit, art too sets out to create a better world and resolutely strikes out in new directions. Once political power is consolidated and institutionalized, the constraints that revolution had abolished are restored, and in fact become more rigorous than ever, for the political powers that be feel threatened by the very possibility that the revolutionary fervor that spawned them may continue. The chains art is forced to bear are now all the heavier because of the greater freedom it has enjoyed. The eternal story of Thermidor is once again repeated.

De-Stalinization should have favored the re-establishment of an open Marxist esthetics. But as we know, the new liberalism was cautiously limited to matters of form. Need we recall that this separation of form and content is contrary to Marxist dialectics? If it is true, as Marxist doctrine maintains, that form, being more stable and less labile, always lags behind content, which reflects historical evolution, but eventually always catches up with it, the contrary may also be true: once form is freed of its fetters, content will not long continue to tolerate its chains.

Should Marxist esthetics retrace its steps and set out once again on the road that led to the revolutionary art of the 1920's in order to speed up this process that is moving ahead all too slowly? Unfortunately, reviving a past period in history does not appear to be possible: a historical climate cannot be artifically recreated. Perhaps Marxist esthetics, a prisoner today of so-called Socialist reality, needs to be quickened by the utopian spirit that Ernst Bloch argues is necessary for Marxism in general in his three-volume book *Hope as a Principle,* that "myth" which Marx uses as a "mediation" between the base and the superstructure and which Roger Garaudy calls in his *Boundless Realism* "the concerted and personalized expression of the awareness of what is missing, of what still remains to be done in those areas of nature and society not yet mastered." In throwing its doors wide open to the visions of a better future and the dreams of freedom that have always comforted mankind throughout the centuries, Marxist esthetics will cease to be the tool of oppression and obscurantism that it has been ever since Socialist Realism became official Soviet policy, and will finally be able to play its real role within a firmly established Socialist society, that of keeping consciences that are drowsy by nature on the alert, of spurring men on toward the ever-widening horizon of the future, of revealing to men the ever-changing and permanent meaning of their existence.

Index

"A propos" criticism, 47
Absolute idealism (Hegel), 6-7, 11
Academic criticism, xii-xiii
Aeschylus, 4, 36
Age of Enlightenment, 5
"Agit-Prop" troupes, 74-75
Alexandrov, G. F., 94, 96
Alienation effect, in epic theater, 104-105, 107, 110, 111-112
Anti-Aristotelian theater, Brecht's, 104, 106
Anti-Romanticism, 87; *see also* realism
Aragon, Louis, 86
Aristocracy, 33, 43, 44
Aristophanes, 36
Aristotle, 51-52; esthetics of, 73; *see also* anti-Aristotelian theater
Art: and Marxism, xi-xxiv, 1-23, 113-117; *see also* dialectics *and* form and content; revolutionary, of the 1920's, 115-116; German (theater), 71-82; Lukacs' criticism of Brecht's, 100-112; Russian, 56-70; under Stalin, 83-99, 116
Art for art's sake, 44-45, 91; *see also* beauty *and* esthetic value
Arvon, Henri, ix, xv, xvi, xxiii, xxiv

"Association for the Study of Poetic Language," *see* "Opoyaz"
Avenarius, 49, 53

Babel, Isaac, 68, 88
Balzac, xxi-xxii, 3, 4, 5, 33, 40, 51, 86, 107, 108
Barbusse, 86
Bauhaus movement, 17
Baxandall, Lee, viii n
Beauty, xi, xvi, 1-2, 7, 43, 44-45, 46, 51-52, 77, 98, 113, 115
Becher, Johannes R., 86
Belinsky, V. G., 14, 43-45, 47, 48
Berdyaev, 65
Berlin, 71
"Bio-mechanics," 60-61
Bloch, Ernst, 116
Blok, Alexander, 65
Bogdanov, A. A., 49, 57, 71-72
Bourgeoisie, xxi, 39, 68; art and literature of, 4, 5, 15-16, 20, 31, 87, 90; Brecht on, 105-108; Lukacs on, 101-104; ideology of, xiii, 11, 32, 37, 47, 50, 56, 57, 63, 67, 72, 89, 93
Bourget, 103
Brecht, Bertolt, xvi, 19, 71; debate with Lukacs, xv, xxiii, 100, 104-112; epic theater of, 75-82

119

Bredel, Willi, 106
Bukharin, 66
Burke, Edmund, xxi

Capitalism, xii, xvii, xxi-xxii, 4, 16-17, 18, 38, 42, 58, 75, 84, 86, 93, 102-103, 107, 112
Censorship, 98-99
Cervantes, 36
Cézanne, 112
Chekhov, 111
Chernyshevsky, N. G., 14, 43, 45-47, 48
Cinema, 20-21, 22, 62, 74
Circus tradition, 60-61
Class struggle, xiv, 10, 39, 69, 71, 73, 82, 84, 85-86, 87, 95, 108
Classic (traditional) theater vs. epic theater, 76-80
Classical period, 30-31, 42, 104; esthetics of, 51-52, 73-74; *see also* classic theater *and* Greek art
Comedy, 36
The Communist, 97
Communist Party, ix, 14-15, 19, 20, 29, 35, 38, 63, 65, 67, 68-70, 81, 84, 86, 87, 89, 91, 92, 94, 96-98, 100, 105, 109; Central Committee of, 20, 68-69, 91, 92, 98; French, vii; German, 72; Nineteenth Congress of, 95; Twentieth Congress of, 96-97
Congress of Soviet Writers: First, 83, 85-86, 87; Second, 96; Third, 98; Fourth, 98
Congress of Theater Directors, 70
Consciousness-as-a-reflection, 49-50, 53-55
Conservatism: artistic, xii, 3, 74, 83; political, 33; *see also* Socialist Realism
Content, 9-10, 64, 67, 77, 103, 104-105, 113; and form, 3, 12-13, 16, 17, 48-55, 110, 114, 116; revolutionary, 56-57, 65-66; Russian radicals on, 43-48; under Socialist Realism, 89, 93-94, 96, 97-98; unity of, Hegel on, 41-43
Cooper, James Fenimore, 108
Cosmopolitanism, 91-92
Critical realism, 44, 87, 101, 105, 108
Cubism, 115
Cult of personality, 94
Cultural evolution, 8, 25-26, 31-32, 68, 93; *see also* law of uneven development

Dance, popular, 44
Dante, 36
Democracy, 101; proletarian, 93; social, 15
Denikin, 85
De-Stalinization, 94-99, 116
Dialectics: Hegelian, 4, 42, 45; Marxist, xiv-xv, xviii, xxii-xxiii, 2, 7, 19, 24-40, 42-43, 45, 48-55, 75-76, 81, 93, 96, 103-105, 110, 114-115, 116
Division of labor, xvi, 32
Döblin, 106
Dobrolyubov, N. A., 43, 47-48
Dostoevsky, 65, 103
Drama, *see* theater
Dubcek, Alexander, vii
Dudintsev, 95
Dutch painting, Hegel on, 5-6, 43
"Dynamic constructivism," 62-63

Economics, xii, 3, 7, 13, 19, 24-26, 30, 31-32, 41, 45, 46, 48, 68, 76-77, 93, 103, 107, 114
Ehrenburg, Ilya, 95, 102
Eichenbaum, Boris, 65
Eisenstein, S. M., 20-21
Eisler, Hanns, 19
Eliot, George, xxi
Empiricism, 28
Empiriocriticism, 48-49, 53
Engels, Friedrich, viii n, 4, 6, 25-26, 28, 29-30, 34, 38, 48-50, 86, 93, 95, 100; on the novel, 5, 31,

INDEX

Engels, Friedrich (*continued*) 33, 36-37; on tragedy and the hero, 9-12
England, 30
Epic, xvi, 5, 8, 30-31, 68, 72; *see also* epic theater
Epic theater, Brecht's: alienation effect of, 104-105, 107, 110, 111-112; vs. classic theater, 76-82; *see also* Piscator
Epinal prints, 89
Ernst, Paul, 31
Essence, 7; and phenomena, unity of, 50-52
Esthetic pleasure, *see* esthetic value
Esthetic value, 72, 77-78, 81, 91, 95, 104, 106, 115; and historical value, ix-x, xv-xx, 1-2, 13-14
Expressionism, 86, 105, 115

Fadeyev, 92
"False consciousness," 17, 32-35
Fascism, 91, 101-102, 105
Fedin, 89
Fielding, 5
Film, *see* cinema
First Five-Year Plan, 68-69
Form, xvii, 5, 8, 30-31, 60, 69-70, 74, 106-108; and content, 3, 12-13, 16, 17, 48-55, 110, 114, 116; revolutionary, 56-57, 65-66; Russian radicals on, 43-48; under Socialist Realism, 89, 93-94, 96, 97-98; unity of, Hegel on, 41-43; *see also* formalism
Formalism, ix, xii, xiii, xx, xxi, 19, 20, 21, 38, 41, 43, 104, 107-108, 113; *see also* form *and* formalist school
Formalist school, 64-65; Bolshevik attitude toward, 66-68, 69-70
France, vii, 4, 30, 32; literature of, 86
France, Anatole, 103
Franz von Sickingen, see Ferdinand Lassalle

Freiligrath, 4, 86
Futurism, 17, 58-59

Garaudy, Roger, 2, 117
Geneva, 16
Germany, xv, 4, 30, 31, 36; literature of, 86; revolutionary theater in, 71-82
Gestaltung (fictional representation), 102-104, 113
Girnus, 21
Goethe, 4, 5, 9, 11, 86
Gogol, 44, 95
Goldmann, Lucien, on genius, xix and n
Gombrowicz, xx
Goncharov, 47
Gorky, 2, 34, 68, 83-85, 87
Gorky Institute of Literature, 89
Great Soviet Encyclopedia, 84
Greek art, xvi-xvii, 6-9, 18, 30
Gropius, Walter, 17

Hamsun, 103
Harkness, Miss, 33, 49
Hegel, 4-7, 9-10, 11, 22-23, 28; on form and content, 41-43, 44, 45, 113
"Hermeneutic circle," xiii
Hero, 31, 76, 111; "positive" vs. "negative," 90, 95; and tragedy, 9-12, 37
Herwegh, Georg, 4
The History of Russian Literature, 84
Holtz, Arnold, 31
Homer, 7
Huysmans, 103

Ibsen, 31
Idea, 22, 41-43, 113
Idealism, x, 1-2, 16, 25, 34, 106; absolute, 6-7, 11; subjective, 27-28, 103
Infrastructure (base), xiii, 25-26, 30, 41, 116
Intellectuals, xv, 32, 57, 93

Jacobinism, xxi, 94
Jameson, Frederic: on Marxism, vii-x; on Marxist esthetics, functions of, xi-xxiv
Joyce, 106

Kafka, 106
Kant, 19, 27-28; esthetics of, 52
Katayev, 89
Kautsky, 36
Kolkhoz novels, 89
Korsch, Karl, viii-ix n
Krupskaya, N. (Lenin's wife), 15

Lafargue, Paul, 33
Language, 21-22, 29, 94
Lanson, Gustave, 12-13
Laplace, 66
Lassalle, Ferdinand: Marx's criticism of, 3-4, 9-12, 37-38, 100
Law of uneven development, 29-31, 92-93
Lenin, V. I., 12, 20, 34, 58, 71, 83, 95, 96; on Party literature, 14-17, 38; on matter and consciousness, 48-49, 50, 53-54, 55
Leonov, 89
Lessing, 43
Lifshitz, Mikhail, viii and n
Linkskurve, 101-102
Literary criticism, xii, xx, xxii, 3-4, 35, 64, 67, 83, 87, 100, 106, 108-109; *see also* literature
Literary individuality (Lanson), 12-13
Literature, xvii-xviii, 4-5, 17-18, 19, 21-22, 29, 32-33, 35, 36-37, 44-47, 57-59; Brecht vs. Lukacs on, 100-104, 105-106, 108-109; of the Party, Lenin on, 14-17, 38, 96; revolutionary (Formalist), 64-68; Socialist, under Stalin, 83-94 *passim,* 95; post-Stalinian, 96-99
Lukacs, George, viii and n, xxi and n, 2, 28, 29, 34-35, 40, 50-51, 52, 54, 92-94, 99, 100-104; debate with Brecht, xv, xxiii, 100, 104-112
Lunacharsky, 60, 67-68, 71
Lyricism, 59, 86

Mach, 49, 53
Malenkov, 95, 96
Manichaeanism, 69
Mann, Thomas, 35, 108
Marx, Karl, viii and n, xvi and n, xxii, 1, 5-8, 13-14, 18, 22, 26-27, 28, 30-31, 32-34, 36, 38-39, 48-49, 53, 86, 93, 95, 100, 104, 116; criticism of Lassalle's tragedy, 3-4, 9-12, 37-38, 100
Marxism, vii-ix; and art, xi-xxiv, 1-23; *see also* dialectics *and* Marx
Materialism, x, 26, 103; historical and dialectical, 8-9, 14, 18, 48-49, 50, 53-54, 93, 112; mechanistic, 16, 25, 32, 53, 96, 103
Matisse, 112
Matter and consciousness, *see* Lenin
Mayakovsky, 58-59, 70
Mehring, Franz, 56
Meyerhold, 59-64, 70, 71, 72, 75
Middle Ages, 42
Morality, xxii, 105; and art, xxii, 36-37, 44-45, 73, 78-79, 90, 103-104
Morawski, Stefan, viii and n
Moscow, 70, 89
Moscow Institute of Philosophy, 94
Münzer, Thomas, 12
Music, 19-20, 22, 62
Myaskovsky, 20

Naturalism, 43
Naturalist drama, 31
Navodnost (national or popular elements), 44, 45, 47
Neo-academicism, 57
Neo-Kantianism, viii
New Economic Policy, 68
Nikolayeva, Galina, 95
Norway, 31; Norwegians, 36

INDEX

Novel, 40, 47, 68, 88, 89, 92, 108; bourgeois, 90, 101, 102, 106-107; Marx and Engels on, 5, 31, 33, 36-37

Objectivity: "Party spirit" of, 38, 44; and subjectivity, dialectical relations between, 10-11, 26-27, 32-33, 39-40, 48-55, 77, 103-105, 108-109, 111-112, 113, 114-115
October Revolution, ix, 16-17, 20, 56-57, 59-60, 63, 64, 68, 71, 87, 105
Odessa, 88
Olesha, Yury, 68, 88
"Opoyaz," 64, 65, 66
Ottwalt, Ernst, 102, 104

Painting: Dutch, 5-6, 43; modern, 112; Soviet, 21
Partignost, see "Party spirit"
"Party spirit" (*partignost*), 15, 38-39, 44, 83, 96
Péguy, 86
People's Commissariat for Popular Culture, 60
Phenomena, 8, 12, 105; and essence, unity of, 50-52
Philosophy, ix-x, 3, 6-7, 23, 25, 26, 29-30, 34, 65, 95, 101
Picasso, 112
Pilnyac, Boris, 88
Piscator, Erwin, 71-74, 75, 76
Plato, 7
Plekhanov, G. V., ix-x and n, xx, 5, 12-14, 43, 45
Plot (bourgeois), 90, 102
Poetry, 4, 18, 36-37, 59, 64-67 *passim,* 86, 109; German, 9-10, 86; Greek, xvi, 7
Politics, 3, 25, 71, 89, 100, 104, 106, 109
Positivism, viii, xviii
Pottier, 86
Pradon, xviii, xx
Pravda, 92

Precapitalist societies: art of, xvi-xvii, 42; *see also* Greek art
Press, the, 15, 38, 59, 78, 92
The Problems of Poetics, 64
Prokofiev, 20
Proletarian literature, 15, 17, 56, 57-58, 102, 104
Proletarian theater, 71-72
Proletariat, 32, 38-39, 44, 61, 63, 74, 80-81, 93, 101, 105; *see also* proletarian literature *and* proletarian theater
"Proletkult" literary movement, 57-58, 68, 71-72
Propaganda, xxiii, 95; art and literature as, 14-15, 18, 29, 45, 59, 60, 72, 74-75, 78, 91-92; *see also* literature, Socialist, under Stalin
Psychologism, *see Gestaltung*
Pudovkin, 21
Pushkin, 44

Racine, xviii, xx
Raphael, 57
"Rapp doctrine," 58
Realism, xx, xxi, 5, 10, 21, 28, 33-35, 39-40, 49-51, 85, 87, 89, 99, 107; *see also* critical realism *and* Socialist Realism
Reality, 7, 42-43, 56, 95; art as a reflection of, 16, 33-35, 36-40 *passim,* 44-51, 54-55, 63, 78-79, 86, 104, 110-112, 114
Red Flag, 72
Reich, Zinaida, 70
Religion, 6, 23, 25, 37, 45, 65, 66, 73
Reportage, 102-104
Revolution of 1848, 10
Revolution of 1905, 84
Rimbaud, 86
Robbe-Grillet, xx
Romanticism, xix, xxi-xxii, 3, 42; German, 46; "revolutionary," 87, 89, 112
Rousseauism, 43

Russian Association of Proletarian Writers, 58
Russian Revolution, *see* October Revolution

Saint Petersburg, 16, 64
Sartre, J.-P., xviii-xix and n
Schelling, 44
Schiller, 9, 10-11, 36, 38, 86
Schleiermacher, xiii
Schmidt, Carl, 29
Schönberg, Arnold, 19
Schopenhauer, 19, 22, 52
Science, 77, 95; and art, as reflections of reality, 46-47, 54-55, 110-111
Scott, 4
"Section for the History of Literature," 64
Seven-Year Plan, 98
Shakespeare, 4, 9, 10, 30, 37, 73, 74
Shchedrin, 95
Shklovsky, 64, 65-66
Sholokhov, 88-89
Shostakovich, 20
Sinclair, Upton, 102
"Social" or "civic" criticism (*obshchestvenny*), 43-48
"Social equivalent of art," ix-x, 17; *see also* G. V. Plekhanov
Socialism, vii, ix, xi, xxiii-xxiv, 16, 28, 34-35, 36-37, 38-39, 58, 63, 69, 71, 72, 76, 81-82, 83-99 *passim*, 101, 116, 117; *see also* Socialist Realism
Socialist Realism, 21, 35, 38, 68, 69-70, 75, 83-99, 100, 105, 108, 115, 117
Solzhenitsyn, 98
The Soviet Union Academy of Sciences History of Soviet Literature, 96
Stakhanovism, 89
Stalin, J. W., 29, 69, 83-85, 88, 89; death of, vii, 94, 95; *see also* Stalinism

Stalinism, vii, xxiii, xxvi, 95-99; *see also* Stalin, Zhdanov, *and* Zhdanovism
Starkenburg, Heinz, 25
State Institute for the History of Art in Saint Petersburg, 64
Stendhal, 86
Subjective idealism, 27-28, 103
Subjectivity, 5, 8, 29, 55, 73, 81; of the artist, 47-48; and objectivity, dialectical relations between, 10-11, 26-27, 32-33, 39-40, 48-55, 77, 103-105, 108-109, 111-112, 113, 114-115
Sue, Eugène, 3-4
Superstructure, xiii, 25-26, 29, 41, 65, 94, 116
Surrealism, 115
Symbolist period, 42
Symbolist school, Russian, 65
Szeliga, 3

"Tendency," the (*Tendenz*), 36-38
Theater: German revolutionary, 71-82, 104-105, 106, 110-112; Russian revolutionary (Meyerhold), 59-64, 70; tragedy and the hero in, 9-12, 37
"Theatrical shock troops," 60
Theatrical staging: Meyerhold's "dynamic constructivism," 62-63; Piscator's, 72-73, 74
Tolstoy, Alexei, 16-17, 84-85, 107
Tragedy, 36; and the hero, 9-12, 37
Trauberg, 21
Tretiakov, 102
Trotsky, Leon, 17-18, 66-67, 68
Truth, 81, 82; in art, 7, 27, 35, 38, 43
Tsaritsyn, 85
Turgenev, 43
"Typical," the, 5, 50, 51, 97

Union of Soviet Writers, 69, 92
United States, xii, xiv, xv

Vallès, 86
Van Gogh, 112

INDEX

Vásquez, Adolfo Sánchez, viii and n
"Versailles esthete," xx
Vischer, Friedrich Theodor, 9-10

Weerth, 86
Weimar Republic, 71, 102
Wieland, 5

World War II, 110
Das Wort, 106

Young Germany movement, 36

Zhdanov, 20, 85-86, 89, 91, 94, 95, 109; *see also* Zhdanovism
Zhdanovism, 15, 91-92, 96
Zola, 86

MARXIST ESTHETICS

Designed by R. E. Rosenbaum.
Composed by Vail-Ballou Press, Inc.,
in 11 point linotype Times Roman, 3 points leaded,
with display lines in Weiss Roman.
Bound by Vail-Ballou Press.

Library of Congress Cataloging in Publication Data
(For library cataloging purposes only)

Arvon, Henri,   date.
  Marxist esthetics.

  Translation of L'esthétique marxiste.
  Includes bibliographical references.
  1. Communism and culture. I. Title.
HX523.A7613   335.4'11   72-12405
ISBN 0-8014-9142-8